The Commanded Blessing

Overtaken by God's Provision
for a Life Without Lack (Acts 4:34)

by
Rod Parsley

RESULTS
PUBLISHING

Columbus, Ohio

Unless otherwise indicated, all Scripture quotations are taken from the *King James Version* of the Bible.

Scripture quotations marked NIV are taken from *The Holy Bible: New International Version.* Copyright © 1973, 1978, 1984 by the International Bible Society. Used by permission of Zondervan Bible Publishers.

The Commanded Blessing
Overtaken by God's Provision
for a Life Without Lack (Acts 4:34)

ISBN 1-880244-17-9
Copyright © 1994 by Rod Parsley
Published by:
Results Publishing
World Harvest Church
P.O. Box 32932
Columbus, Ohio 43232 USA

Contents

Introduction

More and more we are seeing the enemy's work on the earth. Nearly every news broadcast and paper carry reports of satanic activity and graphic descriptions of mutilation. We simply cannot read or hear the news without Satan's trademark being evident.

His tactics are the same in the realm of the spirit as they are in the natural. He seeks to cut off and destroy any part of the body — and the Body of Christ is his primary target.

The ultimate scheme of the enemy is to silence the voice of the Body, cancelling its effectiveness in the spirit realm.

The attack that resulted on Calvary was a blatant attempt at decapitation. But on the third day Jesus, the Head of the Body, beat the enemy; and the entire Body has come forth in new power and might!

Satan learned to respect the Head of the Body, so he has taken his knife to other extremities. He has sought to render the Body imperfect by cutting and radically altering its essential parts. But his plan has been exposed, and the Church is coming together as never before. We are putting on righteousness and standing against the enemy's knife-wielding tactics.

We may have been cut in the past, but we are healing. We are recognizing the power in unity, and we are taking a stand.

For victory...for revival...for breakthrough...we must have unity in the Body of Christ.

Whole and holy, we will lift up one voice in a mighty chorus to the Lord of the universe — and together we will experience the commanded blessing of God.

PART 1 — Unity

1

Understanding the Body

Behold, how good and how pleasant it is for brethren to dwell together in unity!

It is like the precious ointment upon the head, that ran down upon the beard, even Aaron's beard: that went down to the skirts of his garments;

As the dew of Hermon, and as the dew that descended upon the mountains of Zion: for there the Lord commanded the blessing, even life for evermore.

Psalm 133

My preschool-age daughter, Ashton Blaire, had an unfortunate encounter with a door. She was being hurried along by her younger brother, Austin Chandler, who was anxious to get going. In his haste he didn't notice his sister's hand still in the hinged area of the door.

As the door closed, eighty percent of her ring finger was separated from her left hand! Someday — in the distant future — a man will put a ring on that finger (after he has gone through me, of course!).

We grabbed up the severed finger and rushed her — and that finger — to the hospital emergency room.

When I asked the doctor if the finger could be reattached, he began to explain how truly amazing the human anatomy is. As soon as the finger had been sown back on, the regenerative process would begin. Her little body would immediately recognize the dismembered finger as part of itself. In a matter of days it would be as if the finger had never been missing. Each vein and cell would begin to function as if there had never been a separation. A scar would be the only reminder that the finger had ever been detached.

Uniquely United

The human body is a fascinating piece of machinery. It has millions of active parts. Each part is synchronized, and everything works together for the good of the whole unit.

This working unit is the only piece of equipment that has the unique ability to repair itself. Anytime the body malfunctions or breaks down, every fiber of the unit concentrates on the center of the invasion. Lifesaving techniques immediately begin operating to preserve the unit.

When multiple injuries occur, the body's "rescue squad" goes into crisis management, dealing first with the most life-threatening area. Without stopping to consult with other parts, the unit automatically centers on the area of greatest need.

The Amazing Body

Picture this: a pounding headache sends you running to the bathroom for an aspirin. But then you stub your toe along the way, and everything within you rushes to minister to that place of impact. Suddenly your headache is no longer the most critical. It sacrifices its pounding to join efforts with the other cells concerned about that thumping toe.

After hopping into the bathroom, you begin digging through the medicine cabinet to find the aspirin — you need it now more than ever! Then while rummaging through the cabinet, your hand slices across a razor and you begin bleeding profusely. Instantly your body recognizes a life-threatening situation, and it must rush to stop the bleeding for the good of the unit.

Your toe can wait until later to pound and your head-ache can thump another time. At the moment there is a greater need that means the best for your body — survival! The wound must be ministered to without delay.

It is little wonder that believers are to be examples to the world of a body — the Body of Christ.

For as the body is one, and hath many members, and all the members of that one body, being many, are one body: so also is Christ.

For by one Spirit are we all baptized into one body, whether we be Jews or Gentiles, whether we be bond or free; and have been all made to drink into one Spirit.

For the body is not one member, but many.

If the foot shall say, Because I am not the hand, I am not of the body; is it therefore not of the body?

And if the ear shall say, Because I am not the eye, I am not of the body; is it therefore not of the body?

If the whole body were an eye, where were the hearing? If the whole were hearing, where were the smelling?

But now hath God set the members every one of them in the body, as it hath pleased him.

And if they were all one member, where were the body?

But now are they many members, yet but one body.

And the eye cannot say unto the hand, I have no need of thee: nor again the head to the feet, I have no need of you.

Nay, much more those members of the body, which seem to be more feeble, are necessary:

And those members of the body, which we think to be less honourable, upon these we bestow more abundant honour; and our uncomely parts have more abundant comeliness.

For our comely parts have no need: but God hath tempered the body together, having given more abundant honour to that part which lacked:

That there should be no schism in the body; but that the members should have the same care one for another.

And whether one member suffer, all the members suffer with it; or one member be honoured, all the members rejoice with it.

Now ye are the body of Christ, and members in particular.

1 Corinthians 12:12-27

Similarities in Body Structure

The natural body is made up of hundreds of millions of unit cells. A body begins as a single cell that is smaller than a pencil dot.[1] Many cells are so minute that as many as 200,000 could fit on the head of a pin.[2]

As tiny as a cell may be, it has several working parts. One part works to produce nutrients. Another surrounds the nucleus as a type of covering. One part generates energy the cell will use. Another packages protein. Still another transports the proteins within the cell to a warehouse for export.

This warehouse is an important member of the team, housing life-sustaining nutrients. Another transportation division exports proteins that will aid in the reproductive process. A guardian member forms a wall of protection holding the cell together.

Its fortress allows only the escape of waste materials.[3]

All these tiny, seemingly insignificant parts work together in a space smaller than a pencil dot. Their unity eventually produces an entire body and mind with unlimited potential.

Now here sits the Church, the so-called Body of Christ, that should be operating in that same kind of unity. But rarely, since the day of Pentecost, have we come together with enough unity to produce more than a committee. And it is usually formed to discuss all that is wrong with the rest of the Body.

Huge and costly facilities have been constructed for church worship. We can harmonize musically in a service, but that is about the extent of our working together within the Body. The hand wants to be the foot, the eye wants to be the mouth, and the back always wants to be out front. At one time or another, every part wants to be the head!

The "me generation" has produced a bunch of self-centered, self-serving, selfish brats. To the chorus of "I'm on my way to the Promised Land," one church member was singing, "I want my way in the Promised Land." We call ourselves the Body of Christ, yet we have not learned to function as one.

But remember verse 1 of Psalm 133:

Beloved, how good and pleasant it is for brethren to *dwell together in unity*!

A Beautiful Body

When we take communion I always enjoy hearing the song about how beautiful the Body of Christ is. We are to be pleasant — that is, pleasing in manner or appearance — to God. When we are in unity we look great to God.

The psalmist said, **What is man, that thou art mindful of him? and the son of man, that thou visitest him? For thou hast made him a little lower than the angels, and hast crowned him with glory and honour** (Ps. 8:4,5).

That glory is the tangible presence of Almighty God. In the Garden it surrounded Adam and Eve like a garment. They were beautiful to God. They were a reflection of His glory. They were covered with and wearing God!

Then God said to Adam, **Of every tree of the garden thou mayest freely eat: but of the tree of the knowledge of good and evil, thou shalt not eat of it: for in the day that thou eatest thereof thou shalt surely die** (Gen. 2:16,17).

Now when God says you are going to die, He means exactly that: you are going to die. He says what He means and means what He says.

Death is not beautiful, at least not death that has resulted from sin. Once the glory has gone, the beauty no longer exists. Once sin has separated you from His glory, you are nothing but a dirty, stinking hunk of rotting, sinful flesh.

Now the death of the saints is precious to God (Ps. 116:15), but when sin brings about death, God cannot tolerate the sight of it. When His Son, Jesus, took the sins of mankind upon Himself while hanging on the cross, He was suffering and torn. As His blood stained that crudely constructed cross and cascaded over Golgotha's stony hillside, the Father had to turn His head. He could not bear the sight nor stand the stench of the sin of society.

I don't know how long Adam and Eve had lived in the Garden of Eden, strolling the paths in their glorified garments, before they decided to sin. But I believe they had been there a long, long time. I don't think the serpent's deception could have been so effective otherwise. He didn't just slither in that first day, spew a few slimy syllables from his forked tongue, and change the course of history.

The Naked Truth About Sin

Sin is sly. It works much like a cat playing with a ball of yarn. It's fun for a little while. But before you know it, its cords of death will have wrapped around you, and you will find yourself entangled by your despair.

Sin separated Adam and Eve from their garments of God's glory. Once they had lost their covering, the glaring light of reality revealed the bare truth — they were naked! Having been surrounded by all the beauty of the Garden, they suddenly faced reality and the contrast of their ugliness took them into hiding. That slick-tongued devil is still separating people from their covering.

Redeemed and Redressed

Christ hath redeemed us from the curse of the law, being made a curse for us: for it is written, Cursed is every one that hangeth on a tree.

Galatians 3:13

You need to understand what God did through the Second Adam — Jesus. All that God accomplished through Jesus was far greater than what the devil did through Adam.

And so it is written, The first man Adam was made a living soul; the last Adam was made a quickening spirit.

Howbeit that was not first which is spiritual, but that which is natural; and afterward that which is spiritual.

The first man is of the earth, earthy: the second man is the Lord from heaven.

1 Corinthians 15:45-47

The death of our Second Adam (Jesus) on Calvary bought back our clothing, redeemed our covering. This covering would ultimately deliver us from sin and its result — death.

Jesus bought back this covering for you and me. He took that curse into hell and threw it in the devil's face. He has the keys of hell and death. (Rev. 1:18.) Calvary covered it all.

He purchased our salvation with His precious blood, and what He did is greater than Adam's sin. We now have a wardrobe option: we can trade in our filthy rags of sin and death for a robe of righteousness. (Is. 64:6; 61:10.) Because of Calvary we can again be beautiful in the sight of God.

Dwelling Together

I have often wondered what would happen in my natural body if one day my hand just decided it was going off to live by itself. Fortunately, our bodies have better sense than that. The body parts know instinctively that they cannot survive alone. Feet won't just take off because they don't happen to approve of something the tongue is doing.

Unfortunately, the Body of Christ has difficulty understanding this principle of unity. When commitment slipped out the back door, many didn't even miss it. Some Christians were too busy "naming and claiming things." To keep their faith and confession level high, they grabbed their tape recorders and notebooks, and ran from city to city, seminar to seminar, conference to conference. Then when they came home, they just continued to bounce — from church to church.

Daniel, in his prophetic glimpse through the telescope of prophecy, said men would be running **to and fro** (Dan. 12:4). Never in the annals of time has there been such a generation on the move as there is today. People can't seem to be still for three minutes.

In Psalm 133:1 when David spoke of dwelling together he used the Hebrew word *yashab*. To *yashab* means to sit down, to remain, to marry and to endure.[4] So few seem to even stay married these days. If you hear of a wedding anniversary celebration of 25 or 50 years, it's so unique that you feel they deserve the Nobel Prize for peace!

Families used to sit down and eat together at meal time. But now Dad has the bowling league, Junior has Little League, brother has his hockey league, sister is a nurse's aide, and Mom just needs aid! For Junior and Dad to even find time to talk, they have to consult the kitchen calendar.

Things used to be more stable. All the years I was growing up, my daddy bought his gasoline at the same gas station. My mom shopped at the same grocery store. We went to the same church. And Daddy and Mom stayed married! In those days people understood commitment. When they got good service, when they were appreciated and ministered to, they would stay — and not stray!

But so many people these days can't sit still. They are nervous. Everything to them means, "Hurry up, let's go!" God help the sales clerk who makes people wait in line, and heaven help the man who doesn't move his car the instant the light turns green.

> **And, behold, I send the promise of my Father upon you: but *tarry ye* in the city of Jerusalem, until ye be endued with power from on high.**
>
> **Luke 24:49**

Again — but now from the New Testament Greek — we are told to sit down, to settle, to tarry. Only when we tarry will we have opportunity to receive the promise. If we can't *sit and commit* we will never see the commanded blessing of God.

Let's Get Married!

When you dwell — *yashab* — you marry, you make a commitment. This is not a popular message, and the Church gets real quiet whenever it's preached. But if we can't stand to be committed to one other person, how can we even begin to understand commitment to a whole body of believers?

"Well, Brother Rod," people tell me, "I just go where I'm led."

All I can say to them is get the lead out — get somewhere and sit down — dwell, commit!

It has been said that love is blind and marriage is an eye opener. When you date, you take pains to look your best. But just get married and you will learn quickly that your true love doesn't look that good all the time.

Shortly after my marriage, I found my wife in the bathroom plucking her eyebrows. (And I thought they just grew that way!) I can't stand to watch her pluck them. I tried it one time and felt like I was pulling my toenails up through my forehead! But, nevertheless, I have committed myself to this beautiful woman.

Recently a pastor friend was visiting our home. He felt comfortable, so he slipped off his big old shoes. Well, I thought I would gag! I didn't have a gas mask handy so I said, "Put those shoes back on, brother!" I doubt that his pretty little wife ever knew anything about that before she married him. Now, every time she rolls over in bed, there they are — two big smelly feet!

It is the same way with the Church. Oh, yes, we want the glory to manifest so strongly that the priests can't stand to minister. We want blind eyes to see and deaf ears to pop open. We want our family saved. Yet, we can't sit still long enough to get married to one another. We don't want to have anything to do with covenant relationship.

Marriage is a union between two imperfect individuals who, despite their imperfections, make a covenant with one another to stick it out. Too often marriages are based on need.

The Church makes the same mistake. People run to one meeting because they *need* a healing. They run to another because they *need* deliverance. They should forget that *needing* stuff and start *wanting* Him.

We all should go to church saying, "I *want* Him. Oh, I *want* to know Him more." David said, **As the hart [deer] panteth after the water brooks, so panteth my soul after thee, O God** (Ps. 42:1). David knew the joy of commitment. His heart cried that he would **rather be a doorkeeper in the house of my God, than to dwell in the tents of wickedness** (Ps. 84:10).

Be Committed

I am in the ministry today for one reason: because I want the Lord. I want His presence. I want His power. I want His glory.

If we are ever going to have an anointing that will shake the kingdom of darkness, we must learn to dwell together.

For you to dwell in the house of the Lord you are going to have to endure some things. God is looking for endurers. He is looking for folks who will stand at the holy altar and say: "I make my covenant with You, Lord. I will lend You my sword. I am here for richer or poorer. I will be here in the good times and in the bad times. When the storms of hell are raging against us, Lord, I will not jump ship."

The Church has been easy prey for the enemy. The devil has not found it hard to convince us that commitment is a thing of the past. He has offered some appealing alternatives; many have seemed even spiritual or noble.

Diabolical economic conditions have been set in place. You may feel that the devil has forgotten everyone else and has zeroed in on you. Maybe he has pulled your name out of his imperial address book and has your number. Maybe he has attacked your home, your kids, your bank account, your job, your car, your cat, your dog — and even its fleas! You are sick and you are tired — and you're sick and tired of being sick and tired!

He knows that if he can wear you down you won't have the time or the energy to be committed to anyone or anything. He wants you to feel that if you rest for even a minute the roller coaster of opportunity will zoom right past you. His plan is to wear you down so you can't endure another moment of existence.

While the devil is plotting to take you out, God is implementing His plan to keep you in His kingdom.

You are going to stay in the battle, and you are going to make it successfully all the way to the other side!

The enemy is not interested in mediocre and mundane Christians who are flopping and floundering around in what I call "the flatlands of shallow spiritual experience."

The primary problem in America today is not the atheists who are shaking their fists in the face of God. It's not the pornographers who are holding up God's plans and purposes, or the abortionists who are hindering the outpouring of His glory.

The culprit is in the Church.

I am going to preach it loud and preach it strong: *the answer is not in plans*!

I have seen many plans and I've seen many programs. I have crisscrossed this nation and almost seen it all. There are clowns in pulpits, fashion models in pews, and refreshment stands in church foyers. Bus programs and canvassing programs abound. Home cell groups, TV extravaganzas and radio shows flourish. Choirs are trained by the best. Musicians, being paid union wages, are sounding like a Hollywood musical. The Church has it all — but most of it is not really getting the job done.

If you think it is going to work because you have a new plan, it won't. It is going to take God's plan, and He plans to release His power *when the Body comes into unity.*

The Book still says one can chase a thousand and two can chase ten thousand. (Deut. 32:30.) The day is quickly approaching when ten thousand members from the hordes of darkness will be knocking at your door. When they do, it will take two of you in unity to cancel their assignment.

When 100,000 demons take on your community or your child's school system, it will take even more than two coming together in unity to shatter their schemes.

We must unite our forces and commit ourselves to the Body.

As the devil's attacks intensify, our only hope is the strength we have in God...the power that comes from unity!

---

[1]*Your Wonderful Body!* Books for World Explorers, National Geographic Society, 1982, p. 10.

[2]*Amazing Facts About Your Body* (Garden City, NY: Doubleday, 1980).

[3]*Your Wonderful Body!*, p. 10.

[4]James H. Strong, *Strong's Exhaustive Concordance* (Iowa Falls: World Bible Publ.), "Hebrew and Chaldee Dictionary," p. 52, #3427.

2

The Power of Unity

And the whole earth was of one language, and of one speech.

And it came to pass, as they journeyed from the east, that they found a plain in the land of Shinar; and they dwelt there.

And they said to one another, Go to, let us make brick, and burn them throughly. And they had brick for stone, and slime had they for mortar.

And they said, Go to, let us build us a city and a tower, whose top may reach unto heaven; and let us make us a name, lest we be scattered abroad upon the face of the whole earth.

And the Lord came down to see the city and the tower, which the children of men builded.

And the Lord said, Behold, the people is one, and they have all one language; and this they begin to do: and now nothing will be restrained from them, which they have imagined to do.

Genesis 11:1-6

Yes, there is power in unity!

All that is described here occurred with Nimrod as leader of the people in Babel. Those people were in one accord; they had a mind to work — together! The name *Nimrod* means "we will rebel."[1] Even in their rebellion, the law of unity was in effect. The people were determined to reach into heaven, and they were well on their way when God decided enough was enough.

Scripture tells us they were out to make a name for themselves, not to find God and worship Him. When people work together for any cause, there is power in that agreement.

The Dark Side of Unity

The negative force of unity can foster such things as mutiny, insurrection, military coup, mass execution, or blatant lawlessness.

When the National Socialist German Workers' Party (Nazi, for short) came together in unity, more than sixteen million people were annihilated in twelve short years. The Nimrod of A.D. 1933, Adolph Hitler, did not seek to take over the heavenly kingdom, but to rule the kingdoms of the earth.[2]

In today's cities, street gangs have become like family, and their unified force seeks to destroy anyone in its path. Organized crime families have formed such strong codes of unity that even the slightest deviation from appointed tasks can result in death.

... But where sin abounded, grace did much more abound.

Romans 5:20

When the unified forces of darkness come against us, we have a secret weapon: the mighty power of the Holy Ghost. Coupled with the unity of believers we can conquer any enemy.

Defeating the Spirit of Nimrod

Centuries later, the same spirit that operated in Nimrod sought again to control the kingdom of heaven. The devil mustered all his evil forces and marched right into the minds of the religious leaders of Jerusalem. It was a costly move for the hordes of darkness.

I can just imagine the devil pulling an all-nighter. It had been a busy weekend. He and his best strategists were poring over a plan to keep the Son of God in the tomb. But when some idiot mentioned that Lazarus incident, the devil started getting nervous.

Then a sound came filtering through the darkened hall, and when the devil heard it, he was terrified — it was the sound of Jesus, the Savior of the world! Hanging on the cross, He exclaimed in a voice that sent shock waves through the corridors of hell and reverberated up from the bowels of earth, "It is finished!"

The only task remaining was the impartation of the power from on high.

Work Completed, Enemy Defeated

Perhaps the first voice ever to utter "power to the people" was the Holy Spirit as He rode into the city on the very breath of God.

> **And when they heard that, they lifted up their voice to God with one accord, and said, Lord, thou art God, which hast made heaven, and earth, and the sea, and all that in them is:**

> **Who by the mouth of thy servant David hast said, Why did the heathen rage, and the people imagine vain things?**

> **The kings of the earth stood up, and the rulers were gathered together against the Lord, and against his Christ.**

> **For of truth against thy holy child Jesus, whom thou hast anointed, both Herod, and Pontius Pilate, with the Gentiles, and the people of Israel, were gathered together,**

> **For to do whatsoever thy hand and thy counsel determined before to be done.**

And now, Lord, behold their threatenings: and grant unto thy servants, that with all boldness they may speak thy word,

By stretching forth thine hand to heal; and that signs and wonders may be done by the name of thy holy child Jesus.

And when they had prayed, the place was shaken where they were assembled together; and they were all filled with the Holy Ghost, and they spake the word of God with boldness.

And the multitude of them that were of one heart and of one soul: neither said any of them that aught of the things which he possessed was his own; but they had all things common.

And with great power gave the apostles witness of the resurrection of the Lord Jesus: and great grace was upon them all.

Neither was there any among them that lacked: for as many as were possessors of lands or houses sold them, and brought the prices of the things that were sold,

And laid them down at the apostles' feet: and distribution was made unto every man according as he had need.

Acts 4:24-35

On the day of Pentecost the believers were all in one place and in one accord. They had chosen to be like-minded, co-spirited, united in the faith.

The fire of God, in the power of the Holy Spirit, appeared from heaven. It was a sight and sound spectacular, filling the house where they were sitting. First they heard the wind, then they saw the cloven tongues like as of fire come and sit upon each of them. The power of God came, and they began to speak with other tongues.

God gave us a special treasure in the Third Person of the Trinity, called the Holy Ghost. He returned to us the unified language we lost at the Tower of Babel. He intended to return us to one mind — His mind in us. It is God in us Who wills to do of His good pleasure. (Phil. 2:13.)

Then He went one step further: He returned the language that makes us all one voice. He gave us all the same kind of Spirit language — a language no devil in hell can understand and no demon on earth can stop!

Language is the expression of mind and the expression of vision. It is the expression of desire and the expression of goal. When we come together with one mind and one voice, we share one opportunity of purpose — to do the will of the Father. This opportunity was bought for us by the Son and was delivered to us by the Holy Ghost.

Unity is the watch word throughout the New Testament. Though Herod was highly displeased with the people of Tyre and Sidon, when they came to him **with one accord** (Acts 12:20), he was able to make concessions with them. A unified spirit will help bring peace with enemies.

At the first gathering of the New Testament Church they **continued with one accord** (Acts 1:14) in prayer and supplication. When the time of Pentecost arrived they were still in one place **with one accord** (Acts 2:1). The Church continued daily **with one accord** (Acts 2:46), even in times of fellowship, eating together, and in prayers. Deliverance came as the people, **with one accord** (Acts 8:6-8), listened to what Philip was teaching; great miracles took place and great joy took over the city.

When the New Testament Church came together **with one accord** (Acts 15:25) they made some decisions that blessed the entire Body of Christ. The Church was admonished in Romans 15:5,6 **to be likeminded one toward another** so they could speak as one mouth when they glorified God.

Think Alike

Paul admonished the church at Philippi that if they were to receive any of the good things of God they would need to remain **likeminded**:

> **If there be therefore any consolation in Christ, if any comfort of love, if any fellowship of the Spirit, if any bowels and mercies,**

Fulfil ye my joy, that ye be like-minded, having the same love, being of one accord, of one mind.

Let nothing be done through strife or vainglory; but in lowliness of mind let each esteem other better than themselves.

Look not every man on his own things, but every man also on the things of others.

Let this mind be in you, which was also in Christ Jesus.

Philippians 2:1-5

Now, not only do we see how it is God's perfect plan for us to come together in one accord, but we see the importance God places on this unity. I believe we are onto something of paramount importance. The Body of Christ has overlooked it for too long because it seemed too hard.

A Sign of Things To Come

Recently I had the opportunity to be part of an incredible testimony of unity. For some time I had been teaching a message of unity to my congregation at World Harvest Church.

Every Easter our local congregation participates in a "Resurrection Seed Offering." It is a time we all give sacrificially. God gave us His best so we give Him our best.

I believed in my heart that as we gave as a body, our faith would come together and multiply. Others outside our local church body were welcomed to participate as well. As they gave, we would have the power of their unity and would be worshipping together in the offering.

That unity would bring us together in one voice before the throne of God — one voice speaking from one mind, one heart, one spirit. Ephesians 6:8 tells us that what we make happen for others God will make happen for us.

Together we were going to bombard the forces of darkness. I believed we would watch those evil forces fall under a mighty demonstration of the power of God that would be a direct result of the unity of our forces.

I cannot begin to tell you the overwhelming response I received from every corner of this nation. Mighty men and women of God were excited to be a part of what was happening at World Harvest Church.

Many were coming together as never before in support of another ministry. Evangelists and pastors saw this as an opportunity to plant seed for their own critical ministry needs as well.

I received a beautiful letter from some dear ministry friends in Lorain, Ohio. Enclosed with their letter was a check for several thousand dollars. They wanted to be part of the miracle God was going to perform through the unity of the Body of Christ.

They pastor a church of a thousand, yet they were planting seed into a work that was over five times larger. They had complete faith that their act of giving in unity would produce the blessing of God. They even sent a follow-up check to reinforce their position. Their prayer was to clearly hear the voice of the Lord.

Recently they called to report how God had honored their giving and their faith. He was opening doors that the legal system had closed. Located directly across the street from their facility was a prime piece of land. They had been interested in that property, but it was tied up in legal red tape. Besides, a church was not even allowed to purchase that choice land.

As a direct result of their giving, walls began to crumble and the court ruled in their favor.

Now they are hearing and receiving some of God's best messengers into their congregation, and His Word is going forth, bringing life and liberty to their people.

That pastor reported that the results just reinforce what he has long known: you can't give to God and not get blessed. The blessings of God have been both corporate and personal as God has literally opened the windows of heaven in their behalf.

There Is No Foe That Can Defeat Us

When the Church truly comes together in unity there will be no force of darkness that can stand against us.

We all may not have the same theology. We may differ in style and delivery. We each may have a unique vision of what God has called us to do. *But we are standing **together**!*

We have proven definitively that we do care about each other, and the true Gospel is going forth no matter what the ministry name on the door.

A Previous Opportunity

Because of a pure hunger for more of God, unity came to Azusa Street in Los Angeles, California, in 1906, bringing a mighty outpouring of God's Holy Spirit.

A new wave of the Spirit splashed up onto the shorelines of America, and the floodgates of heaven opened with God once again pouring out His Spirit **upon all flesh** (Acts 2:17). The revival lasted until 1913.[3]

That unity brought to us the power of the Holy Spirit with all its fullness which we enjoy today as Pentecostal and Charismatic believers.

The power of God unleashed on Azusa Street literally knocked people off their feet. They were baptized in the Holy Spirit with the evidence of speaking in tongues.

No More "Di-vision"!

The problem with the Church today is we have too many visions. To experience "di-vision," you must have more than one vision. We have to get this thing in perspective, Church. We must get back to the original vision, the original call and mandate of God: to go into all the world and preach the Gospel to every creature. (Mark 16:15.)

Oh, many think they've had a vision. There is the "build a mega ministry" vision. There is the "make a name for myself" vision. There is the "we have the largest television ministry" vision. Most prevalent is the "biggest church in the country" vision.

Ministries today play the numbers game, the name game, and the blame game. Precious few are in the real game — a battle for the lost and dying souls who are without God.

We are down to the last inning, Church, and it is not a game any longer. We are in a life-and-death struggle. If pastors and churches can't even come together to win their cities for Jesus, what hope then is there for the world?

What Spirit Are We Of?

Many believers have become experts at division, the act of tearing apart. Now what spirit are we of? Wasn't it the enemy of our soul who was the original expert at tearing apart the Body of Christ?

Maybe we need a gentle reminder — or better yet a swift kick! It's time for a wake-up call. The Church has been acting just like its adversary. No wonder the world can't tell the difference!

> **Neither yield ye your members as instruments of unrighteousness unto sin: but yield yourselves unto God, as those that are alive from the dead, and your members as instruments of righteousness unto God.**
>
> **Romans 6:13**

This is a battlefield. It is not a recreation room full of video games. We are fighting the prince of darkness who has directed every divisive dart at the heart of our power source — the unity of the Body.

> **For we wrestle not against flesh and blood, but against principalities, against powers, against the rulers of the darkness of this world, against spiritual wickedness in high places.**
>
> **Ephesians 6:12**

When Jesus came, He spoiled the enemy's scheme by covering it with His blood at the Cross. (Col. 2:14,15.) Why then is it easier for us to come into agreement with the devil's plot? Why can't the Church simply come into agreement with one another?

We have been taught the importance of putting on the whole armor of God every day of our lives. We pray the Lord's Prayer, then we get all dressed for battle. We charge out the door dressed to kill — yet instead of a devil-stomping, demon-chasing mentality, we look no further than at one another.

Wake up, Church! You've been doing the devil's work for him. You have ripped each other apart — cut one another open, off and out.

Level the enemy, not your brother. Your hand is not your enemy; your leg is not your enemy; your ear is not your enemy. So stop tearing the Body to pieces!

Have you been yielding yourself to unrighteous works?

"But, Pastor Rod, I don't smoke, I don't drink, I don't commit adultery. I go to church every time I can. I'm not doing anything wrong."

Maybe you have become a "spiritual expert." You know the Bible inside and out. You own every teaching tape known to man. You have fifteen versions of the Bible in your home library. You have been in church all your life, and you are "wise" in the things of God.

In Luke's gospel, Jesus attacks the self-righteous, so-called religious people of His day. He was grieved over the religious spirits, and in that grief He cried out:

> **Woe unto you, lawyers! for ye have taken away the key of knowledge: ye entered not in yourselves, and them that were entering in ye hindered.**
>
> **Luke 11:52**

The root word for *hindered* from the Greek suggests a limb being lopped off from its base.[4] It was the religious people in that day who were the most active in attacking each other, and it broke the heart of the Son of God.

How much more today — as we have experienced the power of the Holy Ghost — must Jesus be shaking His head in agony over His Church.

How has the Church so eagerly yielded its members to unrighteous acts? What have we allowed into our lives to hinder our walk of holiness and our wholeness as a Body?

---

[1]J. B. Jackson, *A Dictionary of the Proper Names of the Old and New Testament Scriptures* (Neptune, NJ: Loizeaux Bros., 1957), p. 70.

[2]*Webster's New World Encyclopedia* (New York: Prentice Hall, 1992), p. 527.

[3]Stanley M. Burgess, Gary B. McGee and Patrick H. Alexander, *Dictionary of Pentecostal and Charismatic Movements* (Grand Rapids, MI: Zondervan, 1989), pp. 31-36.

[4]James H. Strong, *Strong's Exhaustive Concordance* (Iowa Falls: World Bible Publ.), "Greek Dictionary of the New Testament," p. 44, #2966.

3

Hindrances to Unity

Ye did run well; who did hinder you that ye should not obey the truth?

Galatians 5:7

Blame the devil all you want for the wickedness in the Body of Christ. The truth of the matter is — and we must face the fact — we have allowed unrighteousness to rule and reign.

The enemy's work has been easy. He hasn't had to be a very creative thinker. He only had to plant a few strange notions into the minds of religious folks once again.

Failure To Discern the Body

The Church needs to do a little self-examination. The blame game is over. No longer can we declare, "The devil made me do it!"

The holy spotlight of heaven is searching every heart. Some intense housecleaning or cleansing is taking place in the Body. We are being prepared to usher in the greatest revival ever known to mankind. The vessels God chooses and uses will be pure, holy and consecrated.

When Jesus prepared the first communion, He shared the bread and cup with His disciples. He was reminding them that His body would be broken for them and His blood would be shed for them.

> **But let a man examine himself, and so let him eat of that bread, and drink of that cup.**
>
> **For he that eateth and drinketh unworthily, eateth and drinketh damnation to himself, not discerning the Lord's body.**
>
> **For this cause many are weak and sickly among you, and many sleep.**
>
> **For if we would judge ourselves, we should not be judged.**
>
> **1 Corinthians 11:28-31**

The Church must examine itself before it is too late. We want to have a healthy body, yet we don't understand how to begin. Many have never learned to begin by simply renewing their mind.

There are lots of people sitting in church Sunday morning, Sunday night and Wednesday night. They never miss a revival meeting. They purchase every cassette tape and inspirational video. They spend time hearing, but they have left out the second half of the equation. James admonished the Church, **But be ye doers of the word, and not hearers only, deceiving your own selves** (James 1:22).

We are living in perilous times. We must discern ourselves by the mirror of the Word of God and do *all* that it says. As we discern ourselves, we will see the Body of Christ as a whole unit, working together for our good, and for the glory of God.

Perhaps the Church has been a little afraid of the sharp sword of God's Word. It has been easier somehow to allow the devil to cut us up. We have refused to allow the skillful surgeon's scalpel of the Word to cut away the cancerous growths of our unrighteousness.

> **For the word of God is quick, and powerful, and sharper than any two-edged sword, piercing even to the dividing asunder of soul and spirit, and of the joints and marrow, and is a discerner of the thoughts and intents of the heart.**
>
> **Hebrews 4:12**

The Word of God will search you. It will cut away the soulish parts, those that are self-serving and self-seeking. It will expose you, opening you up to the healing and restoring power of Jesus Christ.

Now God doesn't need to open you up for Himself. He already knows you. *You* must know yourself. *You* have to see all that needs to be done in your inward parts. Then you can allow God to stretch His healing hand over every hurt, heartache and hindrance.

If the Church doesn't discern itself, it will die. Once you have recognized your own unrighteousness, you will be open to receive His righteousness. You will begin to operate from spiritual perspectives instead of soulish objectives.

You are such an important part of the Body of Christ. Stop being a hindrance to the life flow in the Body — discern yourself!

Failure To Pray

Moreover as for me, God forbid that I should sin against the Lord in ceasing to pray for you: but I will teach you the good and the right way.

1 Samuel 12:23

Samuel was concerned for the people. They had done great wickedness, but he did not want them to stop serving the Lord. He knew God would not forsake them.

He was determined to see the people fully restored, though they were bent on having things their way. They wanted a king, and they begged God for a king, so God gave them one.

Once the people had gotten their way, Samuel knew they would deserve whatever happened to them as a result. He knew, however, that God loved His people; they were part of Him and He would not destroy them for His name's sake. Samuel was determined to remind God how these were His people and how He should be merciful to them.

Samuel knew he would have to pray.

The people were not wonderful; they did not have it all together. They were not free from sin. They did not do everything right. They were not holy. Yet they were still God's children. They were still a part of Him, a part of His Body. Samuel, too, was part of that Body, and he would not stand idly by and watch them be destroyed.

The Word would later bear out all that Samuel knew God could and would do for His chosen ones. God would keep them from falling. (Jude 24.) Samuel knew his prayers would be answered because God was able to do exceedingly abundantly above all that one could ask or think. (Eph. 3:20.) He knew God would make provision for His Body and would supply all their needs. (Phil. 4:19.)

Samuel knew God could not hate His flesh; He nourished it and cherished it. God would not leave His children out in the darkness. He would not leave His Body sick and afflicted. He would not forsake His people, for His name's sake. Samuel would see to it — he would pray and put God in remembrance of what He had said. (Is. 43:26.)

God is going to take care of His Body. For too long, church members have felt that they had a special obligation to find the dirt of every other member.

It's time we resigned ourselves to know no man after the flesh, but to recognize that every man is fitted into the Body; and that Body is complete by every joint that supplies. (Eph. 4:16.)

You are a part of God's Body!

The Prayer Force

I don't know why we have gotten so far away from a lifestyle of prayer. Granted, the enemy has managed to get us so busy with the cares of life that we feel we have less time to pray.

Prayer is such a mighty force. We are serving a prayer-answering God, but we are no longer a praying people.

If we are not getting answers, it isn't because God has stopped answering prayer but because we have forgotten to ask. He said to ask and we would receive. (Luke 11:9.) We have the power to speak to a mountain with the prayer of faith and cast it into the sea. (Mark 11:22-24.) We must ask!

The last time some of you prayed was when you wanted your favorite basketball team to win the championship, or when you wanted to win the sweepstakes. You want a quick change and fresh oil in less than twenty minutes.

Whatever happened to "tarrying" or "praying through"? We must re-learn the fine art of "holding on" until the answer comes.

How much would we have seen changed in our homes if we had prayed? How much of a difference could have been made in this nation if we had prayed? Prayer changes people, and people change things...by praying.

The Word reminds us that **men ought always to pray** (Luke 18:1) and to **pray without ceasing** (1 Thess. 5:17). We are to **pray one for another, that ye may be healed** (James 5:16). Your prayer may be the key to someone's healing. Plant a seed — pray for someone else's need! When the Body prayed for Peter's deliverance, the prison that held him was shaken and the cell doors were opened by an angel. (Acts 12:5-10.)

Once you have put on the armor of God, prayer is the next required covering. (Eph. 6.) It is time the Church remembered the art of intercession. When we pray for one another, every joint is supplied.

Prayer moves the hand of God. He holds the world in the palm of His hand. If we are not seeing that hand move, we are not praying!

I believe prayer is the greatest untapped resource the Body of Christ has available to wreak havoc in the corridors of the doomed and the damned. A praying Church will kick the devil off his imperial throne and exalt the blood-stained banner of Christ! We need to be praying for each other.

It is time to ask forgiveness. The Body has been a hindrance to the flow of miracles. It is time for the Church to get on its face and repent for its failure to pray!

The Unbridled Tongue

For in many things we offend all. If any man offend not in word, the same is a perfect man, and able also to bridle the whole body.

Behold, we put bits in the horses' mouths, that they may obey us; and we turn about their whole body.

Behold also the ships, which though they be so great, and are driven of fierce winds, yet are they turned about with a very small helm, whithersoever the governor listeth.

Even so the tongue is a little member, and boasteth great things. Behold, how great a matter a little fire kindleth!

And the tongue is a fire, a world of iniquity: so is the tongue among our members, that it defileth the whole body, and setteth on fire the course of nature; and it is set on fire of hell.

For every kind of beasts, and of birds, and of serpents, and of things in the sea, is tamed, and hath been tamed of mankind:

But the tongue can no man tame; it is an unruly evil, full of deadly poison.

James 3:2-8

If we have gained anything from the Word of Faith movement, it should be how to control the tongue. We have learned the power of a positive confession and have developed the art of speaking the Word.

We also were reminded how death and life are in the power of the tongue and were taught that we are ensnared by the words of our mouth. (Prov. 18:21; 6:2.) But this negative side of the dynamic faith message has been generally overlooked.

The positive side has been much more appealing: just make the right confession and we can have whatever we say. At long last we can be in control of our circumstances!

When balance was taught, it was easily ignored. We loved what we heard about the power of the Word, but the rest of the message eluded most people.

The following story illustrates it well:

> There is a story in the Jewish Talmud about a king who sent two jesters on an errand. In instructing them, he said, "Foolish Simon, go and bring me back the best thing in the world. And you, Silly John, go and find for me the worst thing in the world."
>
> Both clowns were back in short order, each carrying a package.
>
> Simon bowed low and grinned. "Behold, Sire, the best thing in the world." His package contained a tongue.

John snickered and quickly unwrapped his bundle. "The worst thing in the world, Sire." Another tongue!¹

The Heathen Tongue

I once heard a story that in the dark recesses of Africa in the tribal village of Kapusha a craftsman carved out a hatchet for the hunt. The axe head resembled the head of a woman, and the sharp copper blade protruding from the mouth of the weapon was shaped like a human tongue. Its creator told the new missionary how that instrument symbolized the most deadly weapon — the tongue!

What that African knew, he had not learned in any university. He did not get his information from a psychology book. He did not get his idea from the most recent TV talk show. For him, life was the teacher; and, even in that remote heathen tribe, the tongue had proven itself deadly.

Sowing Discord

Solomon reported how there were seven things the Lord hated. Of those seven, three are sins that come from the mouth. The first is a lying tongue; second, a false witness (one who spreads tales or gossips); and lastly, one who sows discord among brethren. (Prov. 6:16-19.)

David, the father of Solomon, was a Godly example of a man guarding from deadly, negative, emotional outbursts. He had every opportunity to slander Saul, who had used that young shepherd boy.

But David would not touch God's anointed man, even though Saul never lived up to his appointment as king. David admonished, **Keep thy tongue from evil, and thy lips from speaking guile** (Ps. 34:13).

Speaking Against God's Anointed Leadership

The Word of God shows clearly that there is a high price to be paid for speaking against God's anointed and appointed leaders. One early recorded violation is found in the book of Numbers, chapter 12.

God had chosen Moses to lead the people out of the bondages of Egypt. But Miriam and Aaron, Moses' siblings, felt they were not getting the proper respect for all they had done. They wanted equal credit for being used by God. As a result, Aaron and Miriam were trapped by the words of their mouths.

Another landmark case for keeping one's mouth shut is found in Second Kings 2:23,24. Elisha was mocked, and his manhood was attacked for the cause of his ministry. The *King James Version* reports that **forty and two children** were making fun of Elisha's bald head.

Biblical historians explain how the translation of **little children** in this passage refers to young men of

Bethel who were idol worshippers. When they called Elisha a bald head, they were not addressing his lack of hair but calling him a worthless fellow, thereby making light of his message.[2]

It seems like a quick and thoughtless act, but two she-bears came from the woods and devoured those men with the irreverent, wagging tongues.

For he that will love life, and see good days, let him refrain his tongue from evil, and his lips that they speak no guile.

1 Peter 3:10

Spiritual Homelessness

Another great hindrance to unity is spiritual homelessness. In the Charismatic Renewal, we seemed to get so "loosey-goosey" and so "greasy-gracey" that we did not see as important the need of coming together in our local congregation of believers. We just floated here and there with no sense of commitment to the Body.

But I remember how one day I stood on the auction block of sin. Satan was bidding high for Rod Parsley's life. When Satan reached the end of the bidding, Jesus Christ of Nazareth topped the bidding with His shed blood from the crimson Cross. One drop of that precious blood touched me, and when it did God called me.

Paul said he had been chosen before he was born. He was chosen and called. I too have been called into this thing named "the Church." I didn't just decide to join it like someone might join a local club. I didn't just sign up on a church roll. I was called by the Holy Ghost out of the hog pen of life, out of sin — out of my way and into His way! He called me out of sin into His Kingdom, and He called me into the Church to be part of His Body.

You too are called. There is no excuse for being spiritually homeless! When you are spiritually homeless you have no one to care for you when you are sick. When you have a problem or a pressure you must bear it alone. When someone comes against you, you are alone in the fight. So get planted, rooted and grounded in a body of believers.

Unity Brings Miracles

Recently I received a report of an incredible miracle that came because of this message of unity. I was preaching, teaching and reinforcing this message into the hearts of my congregation at World Harvest Church.

In two subsequent letters with copies of medical reports attached, I received an exciting story of healing. A woman who belonged to my church had been suffering through eight years of steroid therapy and chemotherapy for many bone marrow and blood diseases. "Hell on earth" was the term she used to describe her previous eight years.

As I read about the diseases and the subsequent diagnoses, I could not believe anyone could live in such a condition. A routine blood test — conducted two days after she received her healing — sent doctors into confusion.

In her first letter, she stated: "Three of my family members had already died. One of the diseases I had was genetic. Only God has the power to change our genes and alter our chromosomes. HALLELUJAH!"

After she was tested and re-tested, the doctors could not deny that she had received a miracle. One doctor, whom she had seen for eight years, said he could not explain medically the disappearance of a genetic disease. She knew her healing had an impact on his life.

She had been part of a support group for victims of rare disease. Because of her contacts she could now witness to the healing power of God. She could minister to others who needed a miracle. Her letter ended with this:

"Again, I praise God for the unity of the body here at World Harvest! It was through that unity that I received the anointing of the Holy Spirit that Sunday evening and received my healing! I am now ready to serve the Body of Christ with a healthy body! Praise, honor and glory be to Him that healeth me! I will serve Him all the days of my life because of all He has done for me."

The Body of Christ was in unity. The power that flowed from that unity in the Spirit touched every fiber of her being, and she was restored. Now that is what the family of God is all about!

It is time that we get a home. It is time that we homestead. It is time that we make a claim and settle into a place to become a part of what God is doing in His House.

In unity there is peace. In unity there is strength. In unity there is power. In unity there is healing. There is no limit to what God will do when we come together as the Church, start acting like the Body, and get into unity.

Failure To Return Tithes
to the Storehouse

Will a man rob God? Yet ye have robbed me. But ye say, Wherein have we robbed thee? In tithes and offerings.

Ye are cursed with a curse: for ye have robbed me, even this whole nation.

Bring ye all the tithes into the storehouse, that there may be meat in mine house, and prove me now herewith, saith the Lord of hosts, if I will not open you the windows of heaven, and pour you out a blessing, that there shall not be room enough to receive it.

Malachi 3:8-10

The Church is full of robbers! I know people get tired of hearing messages on giving, but many have never received the message, so we keep preaching it.

Robbers are a real hindrance to unity. A robber takes from a person unlawfully by intimidation or force. He is worse than a thief who steals from people when they are unaware. A robber boldly takes what he wants in a threatening manner.

The storehouse is robbed every Sunday. People come all dressed up, looking so pretty. They lift their hands in the worship service and sing along on all the praise songs. They can have a little tear running down their cheek. They may even dance and shout a little. Yet they walk into church with every intent to rob God of His tithe.

What Is the Tithe?

Though some teach that tithing is off the net income, I believe the Bible is clear that your tithe is 10 percent of your gross income. It is to be sanctified, set apart for God, and brought into the storehouse. A storehouse is a building where goods are stored. It is a warehouse of abundant source or supply. It is the place you go to draw from when you have a need.

You put your feet under the table there and receive spiritual food from every service. You may even get to show off your singing talent in the choir. Your children probably get great truth and fellowship from the children and youth departments — and yet you keep what is God's. You are a robber!

Sunday after Sunday thousands of robbers attend worship services masquerading as Christians, and they are polluting the Body. How can there be unity in the house when some family members are stealing from the very Head of the Body?

Until the Body gets this message, it will be preached again and again. More tape series and books are devoted to this sin in the camp, and yet there seems to be no response. Pastors, evangelists, apostles, teachers and prophets alike recognize the curse on the house that is full of robbers. They have simply been calling the Church to repentance.

Are You the Robber in Your Storehouse?

How can needs be met when there is a robber in the house? The entire Body suffers and the ministry is hindered when robbers line the pews. Church, it is time to stop robbing God. Stop crying and wondering why your needs are not being met. Stop acting like a Christian if you are committing robbery every week.

Most church records indicate 20 percent of the people supply over 80 percent of the finances. Dear God, if this is the case, every church is full of robbers!

It is a hard word, and people don't like to hear it. But if you are drawing spiritual nourishment, godly counsel, training or enrichment in a local church body, you should be paying tithes. If you are not, you are a hindrance to the unity there. Get out or get paid up! You are bringing a curse on your home and on that of those with whom you worship. You have been robbing God!

If you have been borrowing the tithe from God, then pay it back. Pay God the amount you are behind in tithes. And don't forget the 20 percent interest required on all that is outstanding. (Lev. 27:31.)

Do it now! Stop being a hindrance to the unity that God so longs to bring to His Body. Stop robbing God!

---

[1]Paul Lee Tan, ThD., *Encyclopedia of 7,700 Illustrations: Signs of the Times* (Rockville, MD: Assurance, 1985), p. 1422.

[2]Finis J. Dake, *Dake's Annotated Reference Bible* (Lawrenceville, GA: Dake Bibles, 1976), p. 391.

PART 2 — The Anointing

4

The Purpose of the Anointing

To understand the reasons for the anointing, we must first come to know those on whom the anointing has rested in times past.

The first recorded account of the anointing being bestowed by God was the anointing on Lucifer.

> **Thou art the anointed cherub that covereth; and I have set thee so: thou wast upon the holy mountain of God; thou hast walked up and down in the midst of the stones of fire.**
>
> **Thine heart was lifted up because of thy beauty, thou hast corrupted thy wisdom by reason of thy brightness: I will cast thee to the ground, I will lay thee before kings, that they may behold thee.**
>
> **Ezekiel 28:14,17**

Lucifer clearly flaunted his anointing.

What did God see as so vital in the anointing that He would continue the process when He had filled the earth with man?

And thou shalt put them upon Aaron thy brother, and his sons with him; and shalt anoint them, and consecrate them, and sanctify them, that they may minister unto me in the priest's office.

Exodus 28:41

The Old Testament records the first anointing on earth by instruction from God to Moses. Aaron and his sons were to be consecrated — set apart — for the sacred call of the ministry. This anointing would set a precedent for all the kings and priests to follow.

Up to this point Aaron had been a blessing to Moses and had served him well. He had distinguished himself as a man under authority. He was obviously an eloquent speaker because he was the spokesman for the children of Israel. Moses was slow of speech, probably stuttered. (Ex. 4:10.)

Aaron had stood beside Moses in the toughest of times. When the children of Israel were fighting with Amalek, Aaron helped to hold up Moses' hands. As long as Moses' hands were held high with the rod of God in one of them, the Israelites prevailed. When Moses' arms wearied, Aaron stood at his side, steadying his hand until the sun went down. (Ex. 17.)

Aaron must have had order in his home, because God spoke to Moses regarding the anointing of Aaron's sons as well. Aaron was to be prepared for priesthood along with his four sons. (Ex. 30:17-20.)

Then What Happened?

Aaron had been a great asset to Moses and the ministry. He had received the anointing, then.... When Moses went up into the mountain to commune with God, Aaron was left in charge, and he led the children of Israel straight into idolatry! (Ex. 32.)

As mentioned in my last chapter, Aaron had kindled the anger of the Lord when he and his sister Miriam spoke against Moses' wife. Then he incurred the wrath of the Lord again when he assisted as Moses addressed the people in anger. He stood by while Moses struck the rock in frustration instead of speaking to it as God had commanded. (Num. 20.)

Though Aaron was at times full of himself, the Lord had anointed him and used him to stand in the gap for the people. When they rose up against Moses and Aaron's leadership, Aaron made atonement for them with a censer filled with fire from the altar. He burned incense and stood between the dead and the living, stopping the plague that God had sent in judgment. (Num. 16.)

Another Anointing

And it came to pass, when Samuel was old, that he made his sons judges over Israel....they were judges in Beersheba.

And his sons walked not in his ways, but turned aside after lucre, and took bribes, and perverted judgment.

Then all the elders of Israel gathered themselves together, and came to Samuel unto Ramah,

And said unto him, Behold, thou art old, and thy sons walk not in thy ways: now make us a king to judge us like all the nations.

But the thing displeased Samuel, when they said, Give us a king to judge us. And Samuel prayed unto the Lord.

And the Lord said unto Samuel, Hearken unto the voice of the people in all that they say unto thee: for they have not rejected thee, but they have rejected me, that I should not reign over them....

Now therefore hearken unto their voice...protest solemnly unto them, and shew them the manner of the king that shall reign over them.

1 Samuel 8:1-9

The children of Israel had been continually complaining. And they were at it again! Now they were demanding a king. God heard their grumbling and made provision with Samuel to anoint a king over them.

The anointing would be given, but it would come to teach the Israelites a lesson. This anointing would cause them to remember. It would come as a direct result of the people's rebellion. This would cause the children of Israel to turn their hearts back to their first, real and only king — the Lord God of Israel.

Saul's Anointing

The Scripture describes Saul as *a goodly man* (1 Sam. 9:2), not a Godly man, and he was taller than any of the people. (Now there was a man they would have to look up to!)

> **Then Samuel took a vial of oil, and poured it upon his [Saul's] head, and kissed him, and said, Is it not because the Lord hath anointed thee to be captain over his inheritance?**
>
> **1 Samuel 10:1**

Then Samuel told Saul, **The Spirit of the Lord will come upon thee, and thou shalt prophesy with them, and shalt be turned into another man** (1 Sam. 10:6).

Thank God for the anointing! It will do for you what the phone booth did for Clark Kent: turn you into another man — a superman, a better man, a mighty man of power! Yet it is a power that must be guarded, cherished and held in all humility.

The world is always looking for a hero. But we don't need a comic-book hero; we can have the real thing — Jesus!

Jesus also was man — just flesh and blood. Yet He possessed superhuman powers that defied all natural laws. His capabilities were unlimited. When hanging on the Cross, He could have called thousands of angels to His aid (Matt. 26:53), but He chose to die in order to save the world!

An Anointed Opportunity

As Saul left the place of the anointing, God gave him another heart. Signs followed, and he began to prophesy. (1 Sam. 10:9,10.)

But Saul — like Aaron before him — was often controlled by his flesh. Though he stood head and shoulders above the rest and was anointed by God, he stooped to the lowest of the low: he began to allow himself to be controlled by the desires of his flesh.

Saul was disobedient, jealous and full of superstition. He consulted a witch. He sought to murder David, whose anointing he recognized and resented. Finally this man who was anointed king of Israel took his own life! (1 Sam. 31:4.)

David's Triple Dose

And Samuel said unto Jesse, Are here all thy children? And he said, There remaineth yet the youngest, and, behold, he keepeth the sheep. And Samuel said unto Jesse, Send and fetch him: for we will not sit down till he come hither.

And he sent, and brought him in. Now he was ruddy, and withal of a beautiful countenance, and goodly to look to. And the Lord said, Arise, anoint him: for this is he.

Then Samuel took the horn of oil, and anointed him in the midst of his brethren: and the Spirit of the Lord came upon David from that day forward....

1 Samuel 16:11-13

If anyone could understand the anointing, this sunburned sheepherder, David, could. After all, he often had to anoint the sheep in his care for a variety of reasons.

When the sheep became nervous, irritable and restless, it was generally because they were bothered by insects. The flies would buzz around the animal's head and lay their eggs on the damp, mucous membranes of the sheep's nose. When hatched, the larvae then worked their way up into the sheep's head and burrowed into the flesh, causing irritation and inflammation. If left untreated the sheep would panic in fear and run around in a frenzy.

Well, David had an ointment for that! It was not just a one-time application, but a process used constantly to counteract the continuous conflict.

He also understood anointing sheep for infection that quickly spread from one sheep to another. As the animals frequently rubbed their heads together, the disease could spread and infect the entire flock. The anointing cure for this infection was complete dousing of the head of the sheep in medication.

A third type of anointing was needed during mating season. The time to mate brought with it many battles. The rams fought for the possession of the ewes, and the battles often raged for hours. The thud of heads bashing against one another could continue day and night, often to the death. A wise shepherd would cover his rams' heads with grease so that when their heads collided in conflict they would simply slide off each other.

David also knew about sheep growing cold. He knew well the dangers. When a lamb became cold it would often surrender to despair. It would simply give up and lie down, only to die. Shepherds carried a special ointment mixture for this condition. They poured it down the throat of the lamb, and within minutes of the application the animal would revive.[1]

David was anointed by Samuel in connection with his kingship prospectively. (1 Sam. 16:13.) Later he was anointed by the men of Judah, its purpose being to install him as king over the house of Judah. (2 Sam. 2:4.)

In the Hebrew, *Judah* means praise, and David received an additional anointing for praise and worship. As the battles raged, the demands of his life and leadership became greater. He would praise God from his hiding place in the caves when his life was in danger. He would praise Him when threatened by a jealous king. He would praise Him for victories yet to be seen.

Lucifer, the fallen archangel, had been created and anointed to praise. In David, God saw the opportunity for the restoration of praise. This new dimension of praise would come to believers as

David was faithful to the responsibilities of this anointing.

David's third anointing placed him in kingship over all Israel. (2 Sam. 5:3.) By now we should be getting the idea that this guy was God's anointed man of the hour! The task for which he was first anointed and assigned by God, through Samuel's horn of oil, would be an awesome one. David needed a fresh anointing, and then another, to help carry him through.

Though he had received a triple anointing, David suffered human weaknesses as well. The result of his restlessness was ethical and moral failure. The anointing had made a difference in his leadership and even in his praise, but something was lacking in his character.

Two Sons Anointed

David's son Absalom was anointed, but his anointing had come from the people without direction from God. Absalom had gathered the people together in revolt. Because he was handsome and charismatic, people were gullible. He desired to be a judge and set himself up as such, so the people then anointed him as their leader.

Solomon, another of David's sons, was anointed for the kingship, and he operated in great wisdom throughout his reign. His leadership capabilities were renowned and his wealth unparalleled.

Throughout his life Solomon had served God. But as his life neared its end, he began to look back over all he had accomplished. He found himself empty. He looked at life as vanity — all vanity! (Eccl. 1:2.) It was with great wisdom that Solomon noted "stinking ointment" — an anointing that stinks. He said:

> **Dead flies cause the ointment of the apothecary to send forth a stinking savour: so doth a little folly him that is in reputation for wisdom and honour.**
>
> **Ecclesiastes 10:1**

Latin and Greek translations of the word *apothecary* denote a storekeeper, or a keeper of the storehouse.[2] Is Solomon speaking of himself and his life? Did he perhaps perceive that dead flies had gotten into his anointing, the ointment of the keeper of the house of the Lord?

If Solomon lacked firsthand knowledge of sheepherding, perhaps his father had told him of the flies and the death they brought to the animals. Any ointment or food left uncovered would become a victim of the flies as well. Flies would seek moisture even in the ointment and then die there.[3]

Once they began to decompose, they would stink up the very ointment that was to have been of healing and relief to the sheep. Then it was useless. It smelled rotten — it *was* rotten!

Guard It

Beware, all you keepers of the storehouse, guard your ointment. Solomon had already admonished, in Ecclesiastes 9:8, that we should let our garments always be white and let our heads lack no anointing.

Pastors, you can't afford to stink up the house! This has happened so often that many churches should go ahead and change their name to "Ichabod Tabernacle," because the glory of the Lord has departed that place! (1 Sam. 4:21.)

Yes, the flies will still do their best to get to the sheep, but we must keep our oil from stinking, rotting and becoming of no effect. As he is known in the Old Testament, *Baal-zebub* — the enemy, the lord of the flies — is seeking at any cost to destroy, disorient, defeat and cause decay to the Body. (2 Kings 1.)

Elijah and the Anointing

God spoke to Elijah and told him to anoint Hazael, whose name meant "God has seen," to be king of Syria and Jehu to be king of Israel.[4] (1 Kings 19:15,16.) Jehu had been a general in the very army that fought against Hazael. But Jehu had failed in ridding the nation completely of its idol worship, so his lineage was destroyed.

Sometimes you just cannot understand the anointing. It may seem inconceivable that God would anoint the most unbelievable, unreliable Christian you know. You may stand back and wonder if God has lost His senses. But God always knows exactly what He is doing.

We just cannot expect to understand all of the mysteries of God. In the Old Testament God told us this through Isaiah, and Paul reminded us of the same in the New Testament:

> **For my thoughts are not your thoughts, neither are your ways my ways, saith the Lord.**
>
> **For as the heavens are higher than the earth, so are my ways higher than your ways, and my thoughts than your thoughts.**
>
> **Isaiah 55:8,9**
>
> **But God hath chosen the foolish things of the world to confound the wise; and God hath chosen the weak things of the world to confound the things which are mighty;**
>
> **And base things of the world, and things which are despised, hath God chosen, yea, and things which are not, to bring to nought things that are:**
>
> **That no flesh should glory in his presence.**
>
> **1 Corinthians 1:27-29**

Remember, this is the same God who spoke through a donkey. (Num. 22:22-35.) And if God can use a donkey, He can use you!

You might as well face the facts: with all your wisdom, with all your Bible studying and all your conference attending, there will still be things about God that will confound you.

You can't get enough education to figure out God. There are no mathematical calculations that will help you compute Him. No philosopher or philosophy can put Him in a box for you. He is just God, and He will be God all by Himself. Sometimes you just have to let go and let God be God!

A Double Portion

Elijah anointed Elisha. (1 Kings 19:16.) Nothing is recorded about the time or place of the anointing of Elijah, but he had it! It had been so obvious that Elisha asked for a double portion of Elijah's spirit as he was leaving the earth.

The same spirit that anointed Elijah did come upon Elisha. But the gift of God operated differently in each man. Elijah operated primarily in the prophetic, Elisha in the miraculous. Elijah's prophetic word was a fiery word often full of rebuke; Elisha was a teacher who delivered a message of mercy.

The word *spirit* as recorded in First Kings is the Hebrew word meaning "wind."[5] This spirit that was in Elijah was given to Elisha in a double portion.

The Greek translation in the New Testament for *spirit* is similar to that of the Old Testament. Its word *spirit* is *pneuma* and is defined as "breath or breeze."[6]

Anointing in the New Testament

The oil, the ointment, the anointing — all are symbolic of the Holy Ghost. And we *all* need that anointing!

We don't need anymore personality in the pulpit. We don't need anymore popularity within the pew. We don't need anymore "pulpiteers." We don't need anymore slick-haired, shiny-shoed evangelists. We don't need the Hollywood-strutting crowd. We don't need "Daddy Big-bucks" to fund our projects. We don't need flash-card religion or microwave, quick-fix Christianity. WE NEED THE ANOINTING!

Only this anointing can break the yoke of sin's bondage off the Church. The anointing will make the difference. We can't have revival without it.

When the Holy Spirit blew in on the New Testament Church, they were in one room in one accord. The people there were in unity, and the ointment of God was poured out on them. The source of the anointing became intensely more personal, yet corporate.

The Spirit fell on those unified one hundred and twenty who had been waiting in the upper room. They began to speak in other tongues as this anointing overtook them individually. When that happened, the New Testament Church took on a new fervor corporately.

The same anointing in the Old Testament that gave men power to rule and reign again empowered. Men and women received power to witness in every corner of the world. They set about to take kingdoms from the ruler of darkness.

Jesus Himself was anointed with the Spirit of God. In the Old Testament Isaiah spoke of it in chapter 61. The New Testament echoed it in Luke 4:18. That truth was told again throughout the book of Acts. Jesus needed the anointing to accomplish His task on the earth.

> **How God anointed Jesus of Nazareth with the Holy Ghost and with power: who went about doing good, and healing all that were oppressed of the devil; for God was with him.**
>
> **Acts 10:38**

Unique Operation

Jesus healed in a variety of ways. The uniqueness of His ministry reinforces all we have seen in Scripture. The anointing comes in different ways for specific needs.

The one thing certain is the necessity of the anointing for anyone desiring to step into the ministry call. It is critical if your heart longs to do the works Jesus did and imperative if you want to have overcoming power in the age in which we live.

The priceless, precious ointment of the Spirit is the perpetual propulsion of the power of God. You need that anointing if you expect to go anywhere or do anything representing His glorious kingdom.

The Old Testament examples proved clearly to us that one dousing is not enough. David knew his sheep needed continual anointing for many maladies, and he personally submitted to three separate anointings. So he gave an example for us to follow.

Each individual received anointings with specific purpose. The anointing was given for a variety of uses: teaching, leadership, prophesying, ruling and reigning, praising, governing, wisdom and direction, setting apart, cleansing, gladness and defeating enemies.

The anointing is always available. It will be exactly what you need, when you need it, as often as you need it. Maybe you were filled with the Holy Ghost in 1953. It's not enough! Maybe you wept like a baby at the last conference you attended when you received a fresh dose of His anointing. It's not enough!

So what if Evangelist so-and-so laid hands on you last month and imparted the anointing to you? If you went out under the power of God and laid there for an hour, it is not enough!

I don't care if Prophet know-it-all told you that you had it and then dumped a whole bottle of oil on your head, it just isn't enough! You need a fresh touch — a brand new touch — each and every day.

Anoint the Sick

Is any sick among you? let him call for the elders of the church; and let them pray over him, anointing him with oil in the name of the Lord:

And the prayer of faith shall save the sick, and the Lord shall raise him up; and if he have committed sins, they shall be forgiven him.

James 5:14,15

In the New Testament, anointing with oil was practiced in praying for the sick. The Greek word *astheneo*, translated *sick* in this passage, means a feebleness of body or mind, any frailty or weakness.[7] Webster's dictionary goes further to list with physical illness such things as mentally ill, morbid, unsound, tired or weary, longing and in need of repair.[8] Now that hits home!

Ah sinful nation, a people laden with iniquity, a seed of evildoers, children that are corrupters: they have forsaken the Lord, they have provoked the Holy One of Israel unto anger, they are gone away backward.

Why should ye be stricken any more? ye will revolt more and more: the whole head is sick, and the whole heart faint.

From the sole of the foot even unto the head there is no soundness in it; but wounds, and bruises, and putrifying sores: they have not been closed, neither bound up, neither mollified with ointment.

Isaiah 1:4-6

In this passage Isaiah was speaking to Judah. (Remember, *Judah* means praise.) He was speaking to a nation of praisers. It seems as though he was also looking down the corridors of time, right into the sanctuaries of today.

The people in those days were sick, they were wounded and their wounds were stinking. They were covered in infirmity and they needed some ointment. Isaiah knew what they needed — they needed a fresh anointing.

The people of Judah knew how to praise God. They understood twirling and leaping. They knew how to rattle a tambourine. They knew how to sing the psalms of David. They could shout and dance better than any other tribe. Yet they were sick.

Praising provided a temporary poultice perhaps. Repeating poetic phrases lifted the torment temporarily, but a high that comes from jumping around is adrenalin, not anointing. Too much adrenalin can poison your system, but you can't get too much of the anointing. You can't overdose on the Holy Ghost.

What they needed was some anointing. They needed a mega dose of some sickness-chasing, wound-cleansing, life-changing anointing. They needed an injection with the oil of the Spirit.

Sweet-Smelling Spirit

We need a fresh touch of the anointing today. The sweet fragrance of the ointment of God must cover us every day. The anointing is like a spiritual deodorant. It is our safeguard against the attack of rotten, stinking sin.

We need the freshness of the Spirit each day. We need it for our character. We need it for our ministry to others. We need to be the fragrance of life that others will pick up as they pass our way. (2 Cor. 2:15,16.)

The Body of Christ is stinking to the world, and the world has quit coming to the Church. Instead of being a sweet-smelling savor, the Body stinks.

When you are covered with the anointing, you offer a sweet-smelling fragrance to others. Often the presence of the Holy Spirit is so evident you can sense His fragrance. The presence of God can be so tangible that you pick up His scent.

A pastor from Elk River, Minnesota, visited World Harvest Church. He came to receive a special impartation from God. He was hungry for a word from God, and he was waiting for his moment.

Following a particularly spiritually charged message, pastors were called to the front to receive prayer. He came forward and was slain in the Spirit. He knew his moment had arrived. He shared this:

> While I lay there, I saw myself standing in a large, dimly lit room facing an open door. On the other side of the door was something so indescribably wonderful. It was immensely brilliant, almost blinding.
>
> As I stood there God said, "That's the anointing; just go through the door. Get ready, I'm going to pull you through the door today." I began walking toward the door; the closer I came, the brighter the light became and the more intense the Spirit of God became.
>
> Finally I was at the edge of the door. The presence of God was all around me. Then I was through the door; and warm, sweet oil was pouring over me. I was completely engulfed in His presence.
>
> The change in my life was immediately evident. The change in my church is unbelievable. There is a powerful anointing to pray for people. My congregation can't wait for the next service.

A radical change in your life will occur when you get so close to the Holy Spirit that you literally smell the sweetness of His presence. Have you ever hugged someone who was wearing a certain cologne and had that smell to stay with you after you had walked away? Once you come in contact with the sweet fragrance of the Holy Spirit, you will be smeared with it also.

> **Then took Mary a pound of ointment of spikenard, very costly, and anointed the feet of Jesus, and wiped his feet with her hair: and the house was filled with the odour of the ointment.**
>
> **John 12:3**

This was just one of two anointings Jesus received in His last two weeks before Calvary. He had also been anointed in Simon's home. (Luke 7:37-50.)

This anointing was costly, but it was in preparation for His sacrifice. Jesus would need the anointing. He was preparing to go through something, to become the price paid for our salvation. The anointing — it is costly.

[1]W. Phillip Keller, *A Shepherd Looks at Psalm 23*, pp. 114-116.

[2]Joseph T. Shipley, *Dictionary of Word Origins* (New York: Dorset, 1945), p. 1.

[3]Finis J. Dake, *Dake's Annotated Reference Bible* (Lawrenceville, GA: Dake Bibles, 1976), p. 674.

[4]James H. Strong, *Strong's Exhaustive Concordance* (Iowa Falls: World Bible Publ.), "Hebrew and Chaldee Dictionary," p. 38, #2371.

[5]Ibid., p. 107, #7307.

[6]Strong, "Greek Dictionary of the New Testament," p. 58, #4151.

[7]Ibid., p. 16, #770.

[8]*Webster's II, New Riverside University Dictionary* (Boston: Houghton Mifflin, 1984).

5
Costly Ointment

Moreover the Lord spake unto Moses, saying,

Take thou also unto thee principal spices, of pure myrrh five hundred shekels, and of sweet cinnamon half so much, even two hundred and fifty shekels, and of sweet calamus two hundred and fifty shekels,

And of cassia five hundred shekels, after the shekel of the sanctuary, and of oil olive an hin:

And thou shalt make it an oil of holy ointment, an ointment compound after the art of the apothecary: it shall be an holy anointing oil.

Exodus 30:22-25

God directed Moses about the exact amounts of spices to be included in the olive oil mixture for anointing. Now this was a tall order. God expected only the finest and best spices to be used in the ointment. He was specific and His order was detailed.

In modern terms and measurements these directions would amount to 19½ lbs. each of myrrh and cassia, 9¾ lbs. each of sweet cinnamon and sweet calamus, and 6 qts. of olive oil.[1] This combination would be used to anoint the things in the tabernacle that were set aside for holy use.

The oil was also to be used to anoint Aaron and his sons. It was not for anointing just any man's flesh. God declared that it was not to be duplicated or copied in any way. (Ex. 30:32.) The oil was rare and costly, and there were to be no cheap imitations.

Today in the cosmetic market there are "copy cat fragrances," cheap imitations that smell very much like the real thing. The bottles are decorated to look like the original and sold for a fraction of the cost. But the copies just don't last as long as the real thing. They don't have the potency. They lack something that gives staying power.

Many have tried to copy the anointing of God. The devil has created a counterfeit, and folks have settled for that. Many people are simply not willing to pay the price for the real thing. They are settling for less than God's best.

Pure Myrrh

Myrrh may have been the most costly ingredient of the mixture. From its history we find some basic truths about the anointing. Whenever we think of myrrh, it is usually in relation to the gifts brought to the infant Jesus by the wise men. (Matt. 2:11.)

Myrrh — an expensive, sought-after spice — is mentioned a number of times in Scripture. It is widely believed that myrrh was as costly as the gold which was presented to the baby Jesus. When the Queen of Sheba visited King Solomon she brought with her spices that were rare and costly. Many thought the spices were more valuable than the gold and precious stones she also gave. (2 Chron. 9:9.)

Myrrh was used as part of the beauty treatment of Esther. King Ahasuerus was looking for a new queen, and Esther was being prepared to go in to meet him. The purification process lasted one full year. During the first six months she was treated with the oil of myrrh. (Est. 2:12.)

At Calvary, as Jesus hung on the cross, He was offered a painkiller, a drink of wine mixed with myrrh, but He refused it. (Mark 15:23.) Myrrh has a morphine-like effect and has been used down through the ages for medicinal purposes.[2]

At the tomb, myrrh was used in the embalming process of the Savior of the world.[3] (John 19:39.) Its fragrance would counteract the smell of death. Why was such a costly spice necessary?

Sweet Fragrance

In Exodus, chapter 30, when the Lord commanded Moses to make the first anointing oil, He also gave instructions regarding the preparation of holy incense. It should have been obvious by then that God just did not want anything stinking up the place!

When the animal sacrifices were made, the smell of burning flesh would fill the air. The smell of death would be everywhere. So the anointing oil, full of sweet fragrance, had to be applied. With the holy incense in place, there would be no stench in the temple of the Lord. God hates the smell of death.

As mentioned before, Esther was anointed with the oil of myrrh in a treatment lasting six months. That treatment was for purification. The responsibilities of the mandate of God for her life would require her to lay her life on the line. The survival of the Jewish race would depend on her. As she was prepared to fulfill the call of God on her life, she was prepared for death — death to self.

Myrrh is costly. The primary ingredient in the precious oil for the anointing reminds us how we are being prepared to die. Yes, Jesus did die for us. Yes, He did pay the price on Calvary for our salvation. Still, the purest anointing will only come when we die — to self, to our flesh, to our own will, to our own way, surrendering all to God's way.

Yes, the anointing will cover you. It will cover your stinking, burning flesh as it is consumed by the Holy Spirit. As your flesh is incinerated at the holy altar of God, the anointing will carry a sweet fragrance to the nostrils of God — and you will be a sweet fragrance to others as well.

If you are part of the Body of Christ but are stinking up the world, you had better get yourself up onto that altar. You had better let the Holy Spirit douse you with some anointing as the heat is turned up and your flesh begins to die.

Someone once said that the only problem with "living sacrifices" (Rom. 12:1) is they keep climbing down off the altar. When the heat is turned up, they will begin to stink. If they can't take the heat of the call, they "flesh out."

Drop Dead!

Paul said, **I die daily** (1 Cor. 15:31). What does this mean? It means that every day we must die to our will, to our desires. We have to allow all our own hopes and dreams to die.

To me, everything that is opposed to the will of God for my life must daily be laid at the feet of Jesus. I am no longer my own, I am a bond slave to Jesus Christ. Each one of us who hopes to operate under the anointing must *die daily*, as Paul reminded the Church.

God is not looking for more ministry today. He is not looking to lift up my ministry. He is looking for one thing: for Rod Parsley to be a bond slave. That's all.

Sometimes it goes against the grain of everything I know. It goes against everything I want to be doing at this moment. I want to be there in the pulpit preaching like a man from another world. I want to make the people shout, jump, dance and run. But I have to do what God says to do right now.

During a meeting I preached while traveling, the hall was packed and there were plenty of VIPs in the audience. The meeting was going to be beamed around the world.

I had been preparing for days, and the message I had planned to share would have the crowd shouting the house down. I was fired up to preach on the Rapture and the Resurrection, so I was going to hit my best high points.

When I stood up before the crowd to preach I couldn't remember my opening Scripture. Then God spoke to my heart and said, *Are you going to do what I want you to do, or are you going to do what will impress them?*

Daniel 7:9 kept coming up in my spirit. It says:

> **I beheld till the thrones were cast down, and the Ancient of days did sit, whose garment was white as snow, and the hair of his head like the pure wool: his throne was like the fiery flame, and his wheels as burning fire.**

I had never preached on that and had no intention of doing so then. But there I was, quoting the Scripture while pleading with God at the same time, saying, *No, I don't want to say that.* I was in agony. My spirit was at war with my flesh.

From the pulpit I began spitting out words that rose up from my spirit man. I was preaching judgment and talking about a throne of fire with flaming wheels. I was painting a word picture of that horrible day when hundreds of millions will stand before God waiting to be judged.

People began weeping all over the building. Many were looking down at the floor and shifting uncomfortably in their seats.

When I gave the altar call the presence of God was profound. The altar area filled with people who were crying out to God in repentance. I saw deliverance after deliverance.

The voice of God spoke clearly into my spirit: *My power is manifested by what I do when you obey.*

It wasn't my most eloquent message. It hadn't been prepared with hours of research. It wasn't the most powerful word I had ever delivered. But that night I left the auditorium knowing I had obeyed God.

Once we were slaves to sin, but Jesus bought us. Now we are free in Him. In order to serve Him today, we must choose to serve Him. The world doesn't need another gifted man. It is looking for a yielded man, an anointed man.

We are not to serve God just because He made us. We are to serve Him because He gave us the right to choose whom we would serve. We will choose to serve someone. As Joshua admonished the children of Israel, **Choose you this day whom ye will serve** (Josh. 24:15). I now challenge you: choose whom you will serve.

When the heat gets intense and you want to climb off the altar of sacrifice, you need the anointing. When the responsibilities are chaffing, you need fresh oil. When you are stinking up the very house you have been called to serve, you need the sweet fragrance of the Holy Spirit to cover you again.

Myrrh welcomed Jesus at His birth and surrounded Him in death. During His ministry when He was anointed with that costly perfume, it was a reminder of the great price that would be paid. But it also spoke of the great cost of God's anointing.

The disciples could not understand the cost of the anointing. Later they would pay a great price for it. While Jesus was with them, however, the cost was beyond their comprehension.

And being in Bethany in the house of Simon the leper, as he sat at meat, there came a woman having an alabaster box of ointment of spikenard very precious; and she brake the box, and poured it on his head.

And there were some that had indignation within themselves, and said, Why was this waste of the ointment made?

For it might have been sold for more than three hundred pence, and have been given to the poor. And they murmured against her.

And Jesus said, Let her alone; why trouble ye her? she hath wrought a good work on me.

For ye have the poor with you always, and whensoever ye will ye may do them good: but me ye have not always.

She hath done what she could: she is come aforehand to anoint my body to the burying.

Verily I say unto you, Wheresoever this gospel shall be preached throughout the whole world, this also that she hath done shall be spoken of for a memorial of her.

Mark 14:3-9

The disciples did not understand the great price that would be paid. They could not comprehend that their King was soon to die so they could have life. Their ideas of the kingdom came from a fleshly viewpoint, and they each had a personal agenda about their roles when their kingdom would at last be established.

They thought that surely they would need money when they finally took over. When they saw that costly ointment being spilled out, it registered only on their financial flesh meter. Those closest to the Lord could not comprehend His call. But what they could not understand was understood by that woman.

She probably gave the most priceless, precious thing she owned. I have heard it suggested that this rare, expensive ointment may have been part of her dowry. If that were the case, by breaking the flask and spilling out the precious ointment onto Jesus, that woman sacrificed her hope of marriage.

Whatever the actual cost of her sacrifice may have been, Jesus recognized it. Her obedience and sacrifice would bring her eternal fame. Had she paid the price and then poured out the ointment for attention and fame, the response would have been limited. But the purity of her motives brought an eternal effect.

Even in this day as I share her story it is a testimony. Her sacrifice was a memorial to her complete surrender. When you pour out your hopes and dreams at the feet of Jesus, the rewards can only be measured by the light of eternity.

Cinnamon, Cassia, Calamus, Olive Oil

In Moses' days, the pungent odors that came from the cinnamon and cassia were highly sought. They were thought to have some mystical powers when they were used to perfume fabrics. The Hebrew word for *cassia* suggests stripping or scraping.[4] We are reminded to strip off and lay aside every weight that would so easily beset us. (Heb. 12:1.)

Sweet calamus is a reed.[5] The rod of the anointing will break every yoke. (Is. 10:27.) Without the strength of a beam, a building will not stand. The anointing is the structure and strength for the spirit to adhere to and grow. When the true priceless ointment is present, there is balance between the ministry and the message. It is the anointing that teaches all things. (1 John 2:27.)

Because of the thick, gum-like consistency of myrrh, olive oil was added to the mixture. Since the return of the dove to the ark (Gen. 8:11), the olive leaf has been a symbol of peace. When the anointing is present, there is peace.

People dominated by the anointing in their lives are slippery. Like the sheep of David's day they can't butt heads because they just slide off one another. If the ointment is flowing, you will slip right through the fingers of the enemy when he tries to get you in his clutches.

The Price — Persecutions

Then Peter began to say unto him, Lo, we have left all, and have followed thee.

And Jesus answered and said, Verily I say unto you, There is no man that hath left house, or brethren, or sisters, or father, or mother, or wife, or children, or lands, for my sake, and the gospel's,

But he shall receive an hundredfold now in this time, houses, and brethren, and sisters, and mothers, and children, and lands, *with persecutions*; and in the world to come eternal life.

Mark 10:28-30

How confusing for the disciples. Jesus was preparing to tell them of His coming suffering and His death (vv. 32-34), but they just didn't get it. They wanted to rule and reign with Him as their king, and He was talking to them about suffering.

In the entire tenth chapter of Mark's gospel, He was reminding them of what reigning really means: it means sacrifice, it means servanthood, it means selflessness. It is a choice, but we have to choose to pay the price. Jesus was our example as He chose to endure the cross for us.

If you want to reign with the King, it will cost you something.

If you want to operate in signs and wonders, there is a price to be paid.

If you want to walk in wisdom and discernment in your everyday life, it will be expensive.

Like many in the Church today, Peter objected strongly when the Lord spoke of His suffering and death. (Mark 8:31-33.) He just didn't want to hear it. After all, this message didn't fit with his theology.

When Jesus spoke about denying oneself to follow Him (Mark 8:34-38), it was not a popular message. The Greek word for *deny* in this passage means to disown, to separate or depart from self.[6] Self is the biggest obstacle to the anointing. When the flesh controls the vessel God would use, the anointing cannot flow in purity and clarity through that vessel.

Everyone is going to have to die to self. Flesh is going to have to depart. We are going to have to separate ourselves from the deadly devices of our flesh.

Fast Away the Flesh

The best way of putting the flesh to death is to fast and pray. When you fast, you take control over the flesh and put yourself under the control of a mighty God. Fasting will not get God to do something *for* you, but it will put you in a position for Him to do something *through* you.

Fasting can be more than just giving up food. You can fast anything that causes hunger in your body or your mind. You can say no to your body regarding any habit or hobby that stands in the way of the anointing flowing through you.

It takes only 21 days to break a habit. Now I've seen God set a captive free in a moment. But if it takes a 21-day fast, then pay the price for freedom — pay the price to receive a fresh anointing. For some who are bound, it may take longer but the anointing is worth any cost.

When you make a conscious decision — such as giving up watching a football game to go to the local shelter and feed the hungry — that is fasting. That is dying to the desires of the flesh and laying all onto the altar of sacrifice.

When you decide to give up watching a soap opera for a time of personal praise and worship, that is fasting. Whenever you deny a second helping of coconut cream pie, that's fasting. You are telling your body to get ready — you are paying the price to receive and operate in the greatest anointing you have ever known.

When you fast you are sending up some serious smoke signals to God from your altar of sacrifice. You are trading in your fleshly desires. In exchange, you will receive an anointing that will set free those who have been held captive.

Expectation of Vexation

Now about that time Herod the king stretched forth his hands to vex certain of the church.

Acts 12:1

If you expect to operate in the anointing, you can expect to be vexed. The New Testament Church had just begun to operate in the anointing of the Holy Spirit when the spirit of Herod set about to stop its flow. Well, the spirit of Herod is alive and well today!

That spirit of Herod seeks to put a plug in the power flow of the Holy Ghost, whatever the vessel. You cannot hope to escape every tribulation and persecution in this life. But you can have the power to overcome every circumstance when you are full of the Spirit.

Further, in the twelfth chapter of Acts when Peter had been thrown into prison, he was still slippery with the anointing. An angel dropped by and woke peaceful Peter. Perhaps he just needed a little reminder that he was covered by the anointing. When he got up, he slipped right out of the chains that had him bound.

Yes, Church, you will be vexed. There are those who will torment, taunt and try to defeat you. But if you have paid the price for the continuous flow of the anointing, you will slip right through even the most vile attempts of the enemy to destroy you.

Delivered Out of Persecutions

Persecutions, afflictions, which came unto me at Antioch, at Iconium, at Lystra; what persecutions I endured: but out of them all the Lord delivered me.

Yea, and all that will live godly in Christ Jesus shall suffer persecution.

2 Timothy 3:11,12

It is in these refining fires of persecution that the anointing is seen. When you are going through the fire you are being observed by others. As they watch your struggle, they will wonder how you so easily slip right through the circumstances and come out unscarred. You may go to the very door of death, but you won't smell like death.

Like those three Hebrew boys who were bound and thrown into the burning fiery furnace, you will come out of the fire and not even smell of smoke. (Dan. 3.) The world will look on and see the victory in your life. The people will come running, longing to know the secret of your anointing.

Therefore I take pleasure in infirmities, in reproaches, in necessities, in persecutions, in distresses for Christ's sake: for when I am weak, then am I strong.

I am become a fool in glorying; ye have compelled me: for I ought to have been commended of you: for in nothing am I behind the very chiefest apostles, though I be nothing.

Truly the signs of an apostle were wrought among you in all patience, in signs, and wonders, and mighty deeds.

2 Corinthians 12:10-12

When you have been shut in with God, the anointing will just glisten on you.

After Moses had been with God, his very countenance changed. The presence of God changed even his appearance. (Ex. 34:29,30.)

Yes, the anointing will change your life, and it will show on you if you have paid the price.

It Is a Treasure

Again, the kingdom of heaven is like unto treasure hid in a field; the which when a man hath found, he hideth, and for joy thereof goeth and selleth all that he hath, and buyeth that field.

Matthew 13:44

The anointing is a treasure that must be guarded. When you find it, you must cover it and protect it, for it is worth everything. Many want the treasure but are not willing to pay the price to buy the field.

To operate in the priceless anointing, you have to accept the responsibility which comes with the treasure. You may want to show it off and glory in it, but you don't want the responsibility for the field. There is too much work to be done in the field and you would rather run in, show off your gift and leave all the field work to others. But to have the treasure, you must pay the price.

When you are willing to give up everything for the joy of walking in the anointing, you will experience it. When you have laid aside everything that would hold you back, you will walk daily in the very presence of God. When you are willing to work in the field that produces the treasure, you will find the anointing is available daily for each task.

Again, the kingdom of heaven is like unto a merchant man, seeking goodly pearls:

Who, when he had found one pearl of great price, went and sold all that he had, and bought it.

Matthew 13:45,46

The anointing will cost you everything.

All your pride and all your ambition will have to die. Your only hunger will be the burning hunger for more of God.

You will sell out — no matter what the cost — to experience the continual flow of the precious anointing of the Holy Ghost.

Do you want to flow in the purity and passion of your call? Then you must buy that pearl!

The Anointing of a Table Server

You might think that the anointing to serve tables would be less costly than the anointing of a prophet. But each anointing is equally expensive. Stephen was a man full of the Holy Ghost. He was filled with the anointing — the anointing to serve.

Stephen was appointed as one of seven men full of the Holy Ghost to serve on the first benevolence committee for the New Testament Church. The Church chose these honest men to distribute all that had been given so the needs of the less fortunate would be met.

The preachers had been trying to do it all. They were preaching, praying and administrating; and the responsibilities had become more than they could handle. They needed some men gifted with the ministry of helps. They needed someone to hold up their arms as Aaron did for Moses. They needed some armour-bearers who would minister as David did for Saul. They needed some honest men who were full of God. (Acts 6:3.)

Well, Stephen was full of God all right. He was so full of the anointing that as he handled business matters for the Church he began to operate in signs and wonders. There was an overflow of the Spirit that was in him. Passages in the sixth and seventh chapters of the book of Acts tell us exactly what Stephen was full of. He was full of faith, full of grace, full of power. He was full of light, literally radiating with the glow of God. He was full of the Scriptures, and he was full of wisdom. Stephen was full of courage, and at his death was obviously full of love.

When falsely accused and brought to trial, Stephen could boldly proclaim the Gospel. He knew the Word and obviously had filled himself with it. (If you are going to speak under the anointing, make certain you are full of the Word of God!)

Too many times, ministers get themselves into hot water trying to teach the words of someone they heard, something they read, or something they just felt at the moment. We have to be so full of the Word that the only thing that comes out of our mouths will be the Word of Almighty God.

The truth of the anointing on Stephen was too much for the Jews to take. When they began to stone him, they found that they just could not put out the anointing. The very light of God continued to radiate from him at his death.

Stephen's anointing would have a powerful, long-range effect. One day soon after his death, a witness to that event, Saul of Tarsus (or Paul), would receive God's anointing. That anointing would so radically alter Saul's character that even his name would be changed. Before the anointing, Saul was "sought after," but the name *Paul* meant "little." He would become little of nothing to receive everything from God.

From the purity of Stephen's anointing he would bear fruit. He was anointed to bring forth fruit, but the testimony to his true fruitfulness would be fruit that remained. (John 15:16.) Death was never an issue with Stephen. He was going to the Father, and the very act of his death would eventually produce an even greater harvest through Paul.

The Greatness of the Anointing

Great things were happening to the Holy Ghost-filled New Testament Church. Yes, they received great power, great grace, great wonders, great miracles, great joy — *and* great persecutions.

Well, what's so great about persecution?

Persecution draws the anointing to the surface. Whatever may be unseen will come forth and glisten in the light of persecution. When the heat is turned up, the sweet fragrance of the Holy Ghost will begin to permeate the place. The tangible presence of God is manifested in the anointing. At times you can literally feel, see, hear, smell and taste its presence.

Television advertisements for deodorants are constantly reminding us how they really go to work when the heat is turned up. Manufacturers of bath soap have made the same claim. They promise that when life gets hectic and heated, their product will kick in and cover us from our natural, smelly, stinking self. How amazing that these marketing moguls have captured the very essence of the anointing.

Unfortunately, because the Church has not been covered with our heavenly shield, we have started to stink as the heat of persecution has been turned up. God help us to willingly lay down our flesh on the altar of sacrifice. Whether or not we are ready to submit, the anointing is coming on the Church. Only those who have willingly paid the price will receive.

As I watched the news recently I saw several reports of fires around the nation. I sensed that in the spirit realm the Holy Ghost was preparing to turn up the heat. It will get hotter so we had better be covered.

God has a work to do before He sends His Son back for the Church. When the heat intensifies we are going to experience the fire of God. One way or the other your flesh will be consumed.

Now you can continue to stink, or you can invest in some fragrant oil of the anointing to cover you when that time comes. Those who are willing to pay the price will receive of its bountiful treasure. It's coming, Church, so you might as well get ready.

You know that life is going to turn up the heat, so you don't leave home without deodorant. You wouldn't think of facing a difficult day without a good time of fellowship with the bar of soap you consider most dependable. Yet, day in and day out you leave home without the anointing and stink up your world.

No matter how tight money is, you will usually find a way to fit things like soap, deodorant and toothpaste into your budget. One of the hottest selling items in our bookstore before each service is breath mints. People go to great lengths to keep from offending their fellow men, yet they don't understand — or care — that they are a stench in the nostrils of God!

The Cost — Everything!

I once had the opportunity to look inside a small, tattered, daily devotional book that had belonged to an African missionary. No doubt she had drawn strength for difficult days from the words of Scripture and commentary made within its pages.

From Capetown, South Africa, dated 1944, she had made some notes on the flyleaf pages of the book. Where she found the inspiration that she copied, I do not know. I only know that these words, which reminded her of the cost of her anointed call, speak to me today:

> *Awake, my soul,*
>
> *Stretch every nerve*
>
> *And press with vigor on.*
>
> *A heavenly race demands thy zeal,*
>
> *And an immortal crown.*
>
> *A cloud of witnesses around*
>
> *Holds thee in full survey.*
>
> *Forget the steps already trod,*
>
> *And onward urge thy way.*

Inside the back cover of this little book were these words, meant to strengthen and enrich:

> *Matthew was slain by the sword.*
>
> *Luke was hanged on an olive tree.*
>
> *John died a natural death after an unsuccessful attempt to boil him in oil.*
>
> *James the Greater was beheaded.*
>
> *James the Less was thrown from the temple and then beaten with a club.*
>
> *Philip was hanged.*
>
> *Bartholomew was flayed alive.*
>
> *Andrew was bound to a cross.*
>
> *Thomas was run through with a lance.*
>
> *Jude was shot to death with arrows.*
>
> *Peter was crucified.*
>
> *Matthias was beheaded.*
>
> *Paul perished at Rome by the sword of Nero.*

Watch ye, stand fast in the faith, quit you like men, be strong.

1 Corinthians 16:13

That African missionary was a servant of God who knew the cost. When she stood before witch doctors and cannibal chieftains she had already counted the cost. When a python curled around her ankles she had already paid the price.

Death did not frighten her. Why? Because she had already died. She died to her self and to her flesh when she said yes to the call of God. When she laid all on the altar and received the anointing, nothing was left but the sweet fragrance of a life offered up to God.

You can't kill something that is already dead. Dead things don't hurt. Dead things don't run. Dead things don't hide from the threat of an enemy. Dead things don't feel the need to retaliate.

It is no wonder that so few operate under the anointing. Dead people don't need credit for building a big ministry. Dead people don't need to drop names. Dead people don't waste time dreaming up plans and promotions to make themselves look good.

The crippled, diseased Church needs to drag itself up onto the altar. Someone must cry out to God for the sweet anointing to cover the dirty, rotten hunk of flesh that is being consumed there. Someone must be willing to pay the price.

God is looking for a Body that dwells together in unity. He is longing to find those who are willing to give up their personal hopes, dreams and ambitions for the sake of the Gospel.

As soon as the fire is hot enough to consume the flesh in the Church, God is going to crack open heaven, take the oil of His anointing, and pour it out onto the Church like we have never seen before.

Yes, the anointing will cost you something, but it is worth it!

[1]Finis J. Dake, *Dake's Annotated Reference Bible* (Lawrenceville, GA: Dake Bibles, 1976), p. 97.

[2]William C. Martin, *The Layman's Bible Encyclopedia* (Nashville: Southwestern, 1964), p. 549.

[3]*Smith's Bible Dictionary* (Nashville: Thomas Nelson), p. 210.

[4]James H. Strong, *Strong's Exhaustive Concordance* (Iowa Falls: World Bible Publ.), "Hebrew and Chaldee Dictionary," p. 104, #7106.

[5]Ibid., #7070.

[6]Strong, *Strong's Exhaustive Concordance* (Iowa Falls: World Bible Publ.), "Greek Dictionary of the New Testament," p. 13, #533.

PART 3 — The Covering

6

The Nature of Dew

As the dew of Hermon, and as the dew that descended upon the mountains of Zion....

Psalm 133:3

David knew about God, but he didn't really know about dew. He had seen dew, he had felt it and walked in it. He had probably even shaken dew from his hair after a night of resting in the fields with the sheep. What he had never seen, however, was dew falling.

David did not have a fourth-grade science teacher to explain to him the nature of dew. All he knew was that the dew appeared on everything near to the ground. He would naturally assume it had fallen during the night.

Certain climatic conditions must exist for dew to form. The unique process provides a moist covering. In the most simple of scientific terms, dew forms when specific conditions have occurred. When air near the ground cools to the point that it can no longer hold all its water vapor, the excess water changes to liquid. This happens in the early morning hours. Objects that have absorbed heat during the day begin to cool, and dew forms on them.[1]

Dew only forms when the humidity is high and there is little or no wind. When the skies are clear and calm, dew will cover the ground. As the sun rises, its heat evaporates any dew that has not been soaked up.

A Covering

The dew represents a type of the anointing. Hebrew references to dew reflect a covering. When you cover a thing you place something over it to protect it or hide it.

As a child I remember sometimes feeling someone pulling the covers up over me in the night. I had not even realized the covers had slipped off and I was cold until the warmth of the blanket once again covered me.

There was something more than warmth in that covering. When I was covered I felt secure, loved and protected.

It seems like the natural thing to do when checking on your sleeping baby. You just want to make sure it's comfortable and warm. Every protective, nurturing instinct rises up as you are gazing at the little one God entrusted to your care.

You know at that moment there is nothing you would not do for that child. You would fight anyone or anything that was seeking to hurt your baby. You would risk your own life for its life. You would work three jobs, if necessary, to make provision for that child.

You tuck the blanket around that sleeping form so nothing remains outside its covering.

The Anointing That Covers

I will heal their backsliding, I will love them freely: for mine anger is turned away from him.

I will be as the dew unto Israel: he shall grow as the lily, and cast forth his roots as Lebanon.

His branches shall spread, and his beauty shall be as the olive tree, and his smell as Lebanon.

They that dwell under his shadow shall return; they shall revive as the corn, and grow as the vine: the scent thereof shall be as the wine of Lebanon.

Hosea 14:4-7

The Lord was wooing Israel back to Himself. He was reminding them of His covering of love. His dew covered and even encouraged growth. As they grew they would have a fragrance. They would smell sweet because He covered them.

Peter was perhaps reminded of this passage from Hosea when he told the New Testament Church that love would cover a multitude of sins. (1 Pet. 4:8.) David called a man "blessed" who had his sin covered, and Paul announced that statement to the church at Rome. (Ps. 32:1; Rom. 4:7.)

Wings of Protection

He that dwelleth in the secret place of the most High shall abide under the shadow of the Almighty.

I will say of the Lord, He is my refuge and my fortress: my God; in him will I trust.

Surely he shall deliver thee from the snare of the fowler, and from the noisome pestilence.

He shall cover thee with his feathers, and under his wings shalt thou trust: his truth shall be thy shield and buckler.

Psalm 91:1-4

Here again we find the reminder of the importance of dwelling. We are to sit and remain with our God. When we dwell with Him we will find His covering available to us. It is a covering of protection from sin and danger.

Many times David referred to the covering of the wings of God. He had experienced many life-threatening circumstances, and he counted on the anointing to cover him.

He knew that in the shadow of God's wings he could find refuge. (Ps. 57:1.)

He knew he could find protection and care when he was hidden in God. (Ps. 17:8.)

He could rejoice in that covering and he could trust in that covering. (Ps. 63:7; 61:4.)

He knew the shield and buckler would cover his vital organs from every fiery dart of the enemy.

All David needed to do was dwell in that anointing that had been made available to him.

We were created with a covering, and provision has been made so we can be continually covered.

The Anointing on God's Word

Often when dew is referred to in Old Testament Scripture, it is representative of the blessing of God coming from heaven to the earth. Deuteronomy 32:2, speaking of abundance through the doctrines of God, says, **My doctrine shall drop as the rain, my speech shall distil as the dew, as the small rain upon the tender herb, and as the showers upon the grass.**

When something is distilled it is refined or purified. As the Word of God settles in our lives we are washed by it. As that anointed Word washes over our spirit man we are cleansed by it. There is always an anointing on the Word.

The Word has life, and it is the very life of God. The Word delivered from the pulpit is alive. The Word going forth over the airwaves has life. That is why a television sermon taped weeks earlier can reach into the heart of a person who is lying in a drunken stupor in a hotel room.

The living Word cleanses — no matter when it is spoken — transcending time and space.

That Word may come from the mouth of a preacher. It may be produced in a little-known corner of the world. It may be recorded on a video tape, then packaged and shipped to some isolated TV station. At a prescheduled time that Word is placed in a machine. Then dozens of switches, knobs and years of technology combine to transmit that Word over the air.

A depressed mother who believed she could not make it through another day heard that Word and received a refreshing.

An alcoholic who was wallowing in self-pity heard through a drunken haze and was delivered.

A teenager with a gun beside him had just finished his suicide note when that message came over the TV. The noise of that television was meant to cover the sound of a gunshot. Instead, it blared with life-sustaining words of hope.

That is the anointed Word of God — dew from heaven to a dry and thirsty soul.

> **Behold, how good and how pleasant it is for brethren to dwell together in unity!**
>
> **It is like the precious ointment upon the head, that ran down upon the beard, even Aaron's beard: that went down to the skirts to his garments;**

As the dew of Hermon, and as the dew that descended upon the mountains of Zion: for there the Lord commanded the blessing, even life for evermore.

Psalm 133

The Word Is Alive

That message might be broadcast during the middle of the night when every church is locked and every preacher is asleep, but that Word going forth has life.

You may never have seen that preacher before on TV. You may laugh at the way he sings. His accent might even drive you bananas. You may think his necktie is all wrong or his hair could really use some style. But something draws you to his words.

After thinking that way about him, you don't understand why but you sit spellbound listening to those words from his mouth.

That is the anointing. It is the dew of heaven on the Word, the doctrines of God. The living Word comes forth to moisten, cleanse and refresh.

Like the dew, the Word of God settles on those who have grown cold. It settles on the seemingly lifeless objects of His affection who need a touch — those people who are in need of a covering. When the conditions are right, it covers and refreshes.

Weathermen are experts at predicting just what type of events we can expect. They know the dew point, the point at which air becomes so saturated that dew is produced. Likewise, some men and women have become experts at discerning the moment the atmosphere has become saturated with the presence of God. They know when the anointing will be the heaviest on the Word.

A wise minister knows how to usher people into the presence of the Lord. He knows how to challenge the congregation or the TV audience. He compels them to believe in the power of God's Word. But many have tried to capitalize on the power of the dew from heaven for their own selfish ambitions.

Coveting the Covering

And God wrought special miracles by the hands of Paul:

So that from his body were brought unto the sick handkerchiefs or aprons, and the diseases departed from them, and the evil spirits went out of them.

Then certain of the vagabond Jews, exorcists, took upon them to call over them which had evil spirits the name of the Lord Jesus, saying, We adjure you by Jesus whom Paul preacheth.

And there were seven sons of one Sceva, a Jew, and chief of the priests, which did so.

And the evil spirit answered and said, Jesus I know, and Paul I know; but who are ye?

And the man in whom the evil spirit was leaped on them, and overcame them, and prevailed against them, so that they fled out of that house naked and wounded.

Acts 19:11-16

The sons of Sceva attempted to capitalize on the anointing that was coming forth. They wanted to produce their own signs and wonders, and they were naming the name of Jesus.

Sceva was a minister, a member of the Jewish council at Ephesus. He was the chief of priests — a big shot in the religious community! The name *Sceva* means "mind-reader."[2] Perhaps that was his biggest problem: he was operating from his mind instead of from his spirit.

Sceva already had an honored ministry position, but then along came his sons who wanted to look like spiritual hotshots. They wanted the same notoriety that Paul's ministry seemed to be enjoying because Paul was doing extraordinary miracles.

Those men had probably made a study of Paul and his ministry. They may have timed the praise and worship to know just exactly how many minutes were required to set the tone of the meeting. They may have even gone to the local tailor and had a suit made just like the one Paul w~ when he preached.

More than likely they took lessons with a diction coach to learn the fine art of raising their voices at the most critical point of a message. They wanted to know how to draw crowds and keep their attention.

Signs, wonders and miracles were really popular in those days, so why shouldn't they get in on it? They probably rushed to have their hair done in the most current evangelistic style so they would look, act and dress the part.

And they said just the right words — in just the right tone, at just the exact moment — for the greatest impact. If shedding tears was called for, they could do it. If fierce repetition was the order of the moment, they could handle it. They were sure that whatever worked for Paul would work for them.

Well, those sons of Sceva could be working the same way in our modern-day meetings. With the sound system tested and the stage set for the miracle service, everyone would be in his place. They would say just the right words, using the name of Jesus, and *Abracadabra!* miracles would transpire.

They would look great, make a big name for themselves, start a television ministry, and profit from all that hard work — with visions of mailing lists dancing in their heads! Soon they would produce the "Sons of Sceva's Greatest Miracles Video," and they would be known all over the world.

It's the Truth Anyhow

Now you may think this is a little farfetched and that poor Rod Parsley has gone off the deep end with his imagination. But, you know, this kind of thing happens every day. Once some men have seen the dew of heaven manifest itself on a body of believers with signs and wonders as a result, they want to have that in their ministry, too.

The Word says signs and wonders will follow them that believe. (Mark 16:17.) Today, unfortunately, we have put the cart before the horse by following the signs. We want to go where the miracles are happening. We think the occurrence of signs and wonders means that God is there. And, boy, do we ever want to see God! But do we really?

Jesus said it is an evil generation that seeks a sign. (Luke 11:29.) People have been running here and there, looking for a place where the dew has formed. They are checking the forecast trying to assess just where the next occurrence might be.

They are renting buses, reserving hotel rooms and revamping their schedules just so they will be on hand for the next outpouring of the dew of heaven.

Dear God, is anyone willing to dwell long enough in one place for the dew of heaven to penetrate their dry and thirsty souls?

Get Your Own Covering

How can the dew of heaven settle on your life when you are not dwelling in Him? If you want the continual covering of the anointing, you will have to get the conditions right. The dew settles on objects that have cooled.

Has your walk with the Lord grown cold? Does it seem that the Word is not coming alive to you like it once did? You may have felt that you were doing all you knew to do to live right, and it seemed as though you were not walking in the freshness and newness of God.

Even as the dew, His mercies are new every morning. (Lam. 3:22,23.) Maybe it is time to put some covering back in your life. In the quiet and calm of the wee morning hours, the dew comes. You need a fresh anointing for each day. It is time to allow the dew of heaven to settle on you every single morning.

My voice shalt thou hear in the morning, O Lord; in the morning will I direct my prayer unto thee, and will look up.

Psalm 5:3

Wait in His presence. Seek His anointing. Dwell in His fresh and living Word, and your day will be covered by Him.

The Dew Won't Wait on You
Cause me to hear thy lovingkindness in the morning; for in thee do I trust: cause me to know the way wherein I should walk; for I lift up my soul unto thee.

Psalm 143:8

As you wait upon God you will know His will for your day. The anointed Word will speak to you in a greater dimension. You will feel new energy and freshness as you face each day.

The anointing is available. The dew of heaven is ready to settle. But you have to get the conditions right. You must prepare to receive all God has for you.

You wouldn't go to work without putting on clothes. You wouldn't leave your house without combing your hair. You wouldn't walk out into the street without wearing your shoes. It is important that you are covered.

I remember my mother telling me I couldn't leave the house without a good breakfast because that was the "most important meal of the day." She said it would give me the fuel I needed for my brain to function at school.

How is it then that, day after day, week after week, you stumble out into the world without the spiritual nourishment you need? You can't live on last year's anointing, or still be refreshed by last week's dew, or still be empowered by last week's revelation.

Sit still long enough to allow the dew to form. Get your refreshing. Get your anointing for each and every day. God will not force His anointing on you. You will have to clear your schedule. Find a calm place in the morning hours to seek Him — He will meet you there.

I realize that everyone is not a morning person. I know that great discipline may be required. It will cost your flesh something. You may have to go to bed a little earlier.

Do you really want His righteousness to cover your day? Do you sincerely seek to do His will above all else? Do you humbly seek revelation from His Word? If so, then you will have to set aside time for Him.

Have you become too busy to spiritually dress yourself? When leaving the house, are you spiritually naked and vulnerable to every attack? If so, then you have only yourself to blame.

It is time that you seek the freshness you have been longing for. It is time that you stop blaming everyone else for your own spiritual dryness.

Corporate and Individual Covering

When dew covers the ground, it isn't choosy. If the climatic conditions are met, the dew simply covers. The ground and everything on it gets covered by that fresh moisture.

When a congregation comes together in unity, the blessings of God will begin to flow. Miracles will take place. Lives will be changed. Hope will be restored as the refreshing comes.

Real dew from heaven cannot be duplicated. Hype does not bring hope. Dancing alone will not bring deliverance. Magic will not produce miracles. Real refreshing comes only when the dew forms.

People are searching for that refreshing, for that unity. When a church is operating as a body, people will come by the thousands just to experience that refreshing.

Many have been drinking from the stagnant water of society. They are tired and thirsty, and the world is offering them the corner bar. They are looking for a place to rest and refresh. Instead they have found a bar...and bars imprison.

We have the answer, Church. We have the fresh, living water so needed by thirsty souls. The problem has been we have come into the Church so dry and dusty ourselves that we lap up any moisture we can find.

Bring Your Own Dew

Seek your own anointing. Seek your own dew. Seek the personal refreshing that is new every morning. Then seek the lost, the hurting, the dust of mankind.

You can provide the right atmospheric conditions for dew to form. You can help usher in that temporary covering for someone who has grown cold in the darkness of their night. You can produce that clear, calm, moist climate where the dew of heaven will form.

Moisture promotes growth and produces vegetation. Man needs water to survive, so let's get saturated. We can soak it up in the morning hours. The living water is at our disposal. Let's take our fill. Then we can pour out from our anointing on all who are thirsty.

---

[1]*Webster's New World Encyclopedia* (New York: Prentice Hall, 1992), p. 329.

[2]J. B. Jackson, *A Dictionary of the Proper Names of the Old and New Testament Scriptures* (Neptune, NJ: Loizeaux Bros., 1957), p. 81.

7

Covering the Devoted Ones

As the dew of Hermon, and as the dew that descended upon the mountains of Zion....

Psalm 133:3

In the last chapter we considered this verse of Scripture from the aspect of the dew from heaven. Now I want us to look at another aspect of this verse: the place that is mentioned — Mount Hermon — and its importance.

Mount Hermon still stands today on the border of Syria and Lebanon. Though based in the desert region its peak, which reaches 2,814 miles into the heavens, is always snow covered.[1]

When the summer sun beats down on the desert surrounding the mountain, long lines of snow streak down the mountainsides. Some say it has the look of an old man's white hair streaming down around his shoulders. Perhaps the sight reminded David of the anointing oil running down from the top of the head.

When David wrote Psalm 133 he referred in verse 2 to the ointment that ran down from the head upon Aaron's beard and to the skirts of his garments. Many modern scholars and theologians believe Mount Hermon was the place of the Transfiguration.[2] The name *Hermon* means "devoted."[3]

Mount Hermon clearly presents a word picture of those who can receive the anointing. We must recognize that all who are "devoted" have the anointing available to them. When the ancients devoted themselves to something, they made a vow concerning it.

In Latin the syllable *de* adds "in regard to" to a word. Therefore we see that once we make a vow in regard to God we are *de-vowed* — or devoted — to Him.[4] We are His devoted ones.

Other derivatives of the word give us insight to the responsibilities in such a vow process. The word *advocate* is from the Latin meaning "to call to, for, in behalf of." The word *vote* means "first a solemn pledge; then an ardent wish; then a formal manner of making one's wish or intention known."[5]

To devote oneself to God then is to become a votary. One of the definitions for *votary* is "an addict."[6] Those who are devoted to God and addicted to Jesus will receive the anointing from the Holy Ghost.

When you are devoted to something, you exhibit a strong attachment or loyalty. You operate in devotion from a standpoint of affection rather than simply from a sense of duty. You have made a choice to love and commit yourself to the object of your affection.

Everyone who has committed his life to Jesus Christ or ever made a vow to serve God is eligible for the anointing. Why then are there so few anointed? Why are there so few tangible traces of the true anointed of God? Where are the devoted ones?

Lost Love

I know of thy works, and thy labour, and thy patience, and how thou canst not bear them which are evil: and thou hast tried them which say they are apostles, and are not, and hast found them liars:

And hast borne, and hast patience, and for my name's sake hast laboured, and hast not fainted.

Nevertheless I have somewhat against thee, because thou hast left thy first love.

Revelation 2:2-4

In this passage of Scripture John is writing to the church at Ephesus, and yet it is God's Word to His Body today. The Body of Christ has been building, expanding and toiling to share the Gospel. New Christian TV stations are popping up all over, and ministry facilities are expanding.

Ministry support businesses have taken the challenge. Professional printing and design businesses now operate solely to facilitate the phenomenal growth of mega ministries. It is big business and growing every day.

New churches are continually being constructed in this country. Hundreds of ministers are ordained each year. There seems to be no shortage of ministries or ministers, but there is certainly a shortage of the anointing.

The Church has become professional in doing the work of the Lord, but it has forgotten the Lord of the work! We have more religion than we know what to do with. What God wants from us is not religion, but relationship.

Maybe you have worked hard. You have been faithful in your church attendance. You have involved yourself in every good project that presented itself. But now you are longing for more. All your best efforts don't seem to be making a bit of difference.

You long to see miracles. You want to be used of God to set someone free from their bondages. You want your church services to be power packed. You want to hear preaching that will convict and bring change.

A renewed love relationship will bring the anointing, but this relationship will take work.

Now you may say, "But, Pastor Rod, I've been working. I'm on every committee in my church. I drive a bus on Sundays and work with the youth on Wednesday nights. On Saturdays I go to a nursing home and teach a Bible study. I'm already so busy; I don't have time for more work."

Yes, you are doing all the right things, but you have lost your relationship.

When a husband is too busy working just to provide for the physical needs of his family, he may fail to meet their emotional needs. When he is always at the office or off on a business trip, he may think he is doing everything to provide. But he is never at home.

Then when he is home, he is too tired to notice his child's need to be held. He is too exhausted from all his labors to hold his wife and listen to the cares of her day. The very thing he is working to provide for may be slipping right through his fingers. He needs to renew his relationship.

A wife can become completely engrossed in the children's activities and in the responsibilities of caring for the home. She can exhaust herself running a taxi service to all the school events and shopping for the family's needs. Then when it comes time for relationship she's just too tired. It's just not important anymore.

What happens then is that the very thing which has been the foundation of this lifestyle — the relationship — is in shambles. If the relationship is not rekindled, the home and the family can easily be lost. If effort is not made to maintain the original devotion, the entire unit is threatened.

This scenario topples lives and ministries every day. People seem to have forgotten their basic motivation for what they were building. They have lost their first love and have forgotten their vows.

Get Addicted

Do you remember how you felt the first time you fell in love? There is a lesson to be learned from your trip down memory lane.

When you first fell in love you couldn't stand to be apart from the object of your devotion. You wanted to be with her every waking moment of the day — looking into her eyes, holding her hand, talking to her.

You would plan, plot and scheme to find any excuse to see the one you loved. There were few obstacles that were insurmountable. Even if both of you were working at a job, you would make time to spend together.

You could go without sleep indefinitely and would even forget to eat. Your mind would constantly be wrapped up with thoughts of the one you loved. Everything you did had new purpose and meaning. No longer did you brush your teeth to fight cavities — you did it for the one you adored!

When finances were a problem, you would scrimp, save, even do without things yourself. You would make a way to take her on a nice date or buy her a present. Just the mention of that special name would make your heart race. You were hooked!

During that time you were addicted. You could never get enough of being with that one. You wore the tires off your car running back and forth so you could be together. You would spend hundreds of dollars on long-distance phone calls, if necessary, because you were devoted.

You would have paid whatever the price just to be near the one you loved. Money was no object, distance was no problem, time didn't matter, and sleep wasn't important. No sacrifice was too great. You would do whatever it took to support your "habit." Each "fix" just left you wanting more.

Addictions are costly. Anything you are devoted to will cost you something. A car buff spends hours working on the object of his affection. He forgets his other responsibilities and will work until the wee hours of the morning fixing up his treasure. He spends hours on end, scouring junkyards for just the right part. No matter what the price, that part must be exact. He will see to every detail, from the upholstery to the taillights. No expense is spared. He is consumed with that piece of machinery.

Addicted to Jesus

Look now down another avenue of memory. Remember the day, the hour, the very moment you gave your heart to Jesus. Your heart was so full of love you thought it would burst. You couldn't get enough of being in His presence. You longed for His Word. You ached to know Him more.

When I was a child, I loved to be around preachers. I'd get as close to them as I could, and stay as long as I could.

I would often wrap my arms and legs around my pastor's legs and hold on. He'd just let me stay there and would walk along, dragging me as he went!

I now know I was drawn to the anointing.

When I got saved I didn't need someone from the church visitation committee for "follow-up." I was hooked — absolutely addicted — to Jesus. I couldn't wait for the next opportunity to go to church. I searched the newspaper for revivals or special meetings going on anywhere, and then begged my parents to take me.

I never became tired of being in His presence or of hearing His Word. I was devoted. I felt an unquenchable passion for more of Him and vowed to serve Him the rest of my life. I would stay connected no matter what the cost.

In the Levitical Law, God spoke to Moses in regard to the vows. (Lev. 27.) Each vow had an offering attached. There was a price to be paid for each item devoted to God.

The same is true today. Although a vow is voluntary, there is a price attached. Anything to which you devote yourself will cost you something.

Now, I want to remind you that salvation is free. Jesus paid the price for it on Calvary. Because of that price, we can receive the gift of eternal life and the blood's atonement for our sins.

Once we make a commitment to serve the Lord all the days of our lives, we need the anointing. We need the precious oil of the Holy Ghost — and that will cost us something.

Devoted or Detached

I am the true vine, and my Father is the husbandman.

Every branch in me that beareth not fruit he taketh away: and every branch that beareth fruit, he purgeth it, that it may bring forth more fruit.

Now ye are clean through the word which I have spoken unto you.

Abide in me, and I in you. As the branch cannot bear fruit of itself, except it abide in the vine; no more can ye, except ye abide in me.

I am the vine, ye are the branches: He that abideth in me, and I in him, the same bringeth forth much fruit: for without me ye can do nothing.

John 15:1-5

We are hooked — grafted in — to the Vine. We can't live without life coming from our Source. That desire in you, crying to be fruitful, can only be satisfied by dwelling in the Vine.

For if the firstfruit be holy, the lump is also holy: and if the root be holy, so are the branches.

And if some of the branches be broken off, and thou, being a wild olive tree, wert grafted in among them, and with them partakest of the root and fatness of the olive tree;

Boast not against the branches. But if thou boast, thou bearest not the root, but the root thee.

Thou wilt say then, The branches were broken off, that I might be grafted in.

Well; because of unbelief they were broken off, and thou standest by faith. Be not highminded, but fear:

For if God spared not the natural branches, take heed lest he also spare not thee.

Behold therefore the goodness and severity of God: on them which fell, severity; but toward thee, goodness, if thou continue in his goodness: otherwise thou also shalt be cut off.

And they also, if they abide not still in unbelief, shall be grafted in: for God is able to graft them in again.

For if thou wert cut out of the olive tree which is wild by nature, and wert grafted contrary to nature into a good olive tree: how much more shall these, which be the natural branches, be grafted into their own olive tree?

Romans 11:16-24

Who Moved?

A man and his wife were riding along one day in their car. The wife decided it was time they had a long-overdue talk about their relationship. She had tried on other occasions, but the husband had always seemed too busy or escaped to a project needing to be done around the house.

That day she had a captive audience. They were on a long stretch of highway and he had nowhere to run. She began by asking him the question, "What has happened to our relationship?"

Without slowing down to allow him to answer, she started listing all the things they once enjoyed doing together. She reminded him just how long it had been since they had done any of those things. To her they were like ships passing in the night. They shared the same bed, but for the other sixteen hours of the day they were rarely together.

She was about to end her tirade when one last brilliant thought came to mind. This would emphasize all she had been saying. "Just look at us," she said, "we don't even sit next to each other in the car anymore."

The man of few words took a long look across the front seat at her and said, "Well, I'm not the one who moved."

When we, the branches, become detached from the Vine, generally it is our own fault. The Vine does not leave its branches; we choose to become detached from Him. We allow our flesh and the devil's devices to bring division in our relationship to the Vine. He has not lost His devotion to us.

Have you moved — pulled away — from Him? You may have allowed sin to separate you from the Vine. You may have been lopped off by a vicious attack of the enemy. Remember, as we learned in chapter 2, "di-vision" is his specialty.

Whatever the interruption may be, you can become detached from the Vine. If you no longer feel the life flow of the anointing of the Vine, it is because you have been disconnected. But, remember, He still loves you. You are still His devoted, even if you have moved away from that devotion.

When detached, you were separated from the life source of your spirit man. Without that life flow, your spiritual branch can dry and shrivel up. You can become indifferent or disinterested in the things of God.

Through salvation we are grafted into this Vine — adopted into the family of God — to become a part of His life source. As soon as the graft process is completed, you can't tell the grafted branch from one that grew there on its own.

When you were grafted into the kingdom of God, you became united with the Vine. Much like a transplanted organ you began to function as a normal part of the Vine. Soon after, your body could not even remember that you were once part of another. You became united and one with your new source of life flow.

When Jesus spoke to the religious people of His day, He spoke in terms they could understand. When those in the church at Rome were reminded of their opportunity to be part of the Vine, they would never have understood the transplant but they could understand the process of grafting.

The Jews were the original branches that grew on the Vine. Now we have been offered the opportunity to be grafted in — to be adopted — by God. Everything that was offered to the Jews has been opened and made available to us. Once we are adopted into the family we are able to look like, act like and talk like the Father, because His life now actually flows through our being.

When we become like our Father, we will operate in His power. The same power that flows through Him flows through us by the Holy Ghost. We now have the ability to do the same miracles Jesus did.

We have the power to live victoriously. We have the power to overcome the world. We have legal access to anything God has. He is our Father. We are part of Him. We are united. We have been grafted in. We are His devoted.

It is time you — the devoted — recognized your place. It is time you recognized your power source. If you are not attached, it is time to get grafted in. It is time to make that commitment: to become devoted to the Vine, Jesus Christ.

You need His power source — the anointing of the Holy Ghost — in your life. You are His devoted. You are part of the family of God. You are an essential part of the Vine. You are a critical part of the Body of Christ.

Holy Husbandry

If God has called and ordained you to a place of leadership in His Body, then you are in the business of husbandry. You are to carefully, thoughtfully and skillfully manage the grafted branches, insuring that the graft takes.

Much as the transplant surgeon watches a patient closely to guard against rejection, you guard the grafted branches. It is your responsibility before God to manage those who have only recently become attached.

While ministering in South Africa, I received a prophetic word. As I was walking through the lobby of the hotel in Johannesburg, a stranger approached. He said he had a word from the Lord for me.

Personal prophecy is not directional but confirmational. In other words, personal prophecy should not tell you what to do; it should confirm what God has already been speaking to your heart.

My ears perked up when the man said: "May I share this word with you? You can put it before the Lord. You can share it with your elders. You can put it before your pastor and judge it." When he had said that, I knew he was on track.

He proceeded then to give me this word: "They shall call you Mahanian."

Well, I have been called a lot of things in my life, but that was a new one on me.

"What does *Mahanian* mean?" I asked.

He replied, "It means the joiner of separate camps into one."

He continued by explaining how God would use the ministry He had given me as a hub of a wheel whose spokes would reach out to others. It would unite many who were reaching out in one voice, one spirit, one mind and one purpose.

The responsibility of the priest is to bring people to God. He oversees the sacrifices of the people. He is responsible for receiving their sacrifices and taking them to God.

We are operating in this priestly anointing. We each have a responsibility as kings and priests unto God. (Rev. 1:6.) We each are the devoted of God. This anointing is available to us to help bring the people to God — to unite His Body once again. As we offer Him this sacrifice of unity in the Body, He will rend the heavens and come down.

God longs for His Church to come together. If we do not know our place or recognize our devotion to the Body, how will we be able to recognize the place of another? We are to be the devoted ones, the object of His love.

God wants to cover you with His precious, priceless anointing. He longs to cover His devoted. He has placed you and positioned you to be part of this Body — part of His devoted ones.

[1]*Webster's New World Encyclopedia* (New York: Prentice Hall, 1992), p. 520.

[2]*The System Bible Study* (Chicago: John Rudin, 1971), p. 166.

[3]J. B. Jackson, *A Dictionary of the Proper Names of the Old and New Testament Scriptures* (Neptune, NJ: Loizeaux Bros., 1957), p. 41.

[4]Joseph T. Shipley, *Dictionary of Word Origins* (New York: Dorset, 1945), p. 382.

[5]Ibid.

[6]*Webster's Third New International Dictionary*, Merriam-Webster, Inc., 1986, p. 2565.

8

A Place Called *There*

It is like the precious ointment upon the head,
that ran down upon the beard, even Aaron's beard:
that went down to the skirts of his garments;

As the dew of Hermon, and as the dew that
descended upon the mountains of Zion: for *there*
the Lord commanded the blessing, even life for
evermore.

Psalm 133:2,3

In this psalm, David illustrates unity with some
colorful word pictures. The pictures we see,
however, have great spiritual significance.

It is easy to skip over the depth of truth buried in
these verses and run right to *there*. Everyone wants
to know how to get to where the blessing will be
commanded upon them by God. So the big question
is, "Where is *there*?"

We have already found how the ointment and
the dew are types of the anointing. When the
anointing comes, it manifests itself in four different
places, as referred to in verses 2 and 3 of this psalm.
It came first on Aaron's **head**; then it ran down upon
his **beard**; next it flowed down the skirts of his
garments; and, lastly, it descended upon **Zion**.

The anointing is an amazing and almost elusive thing. It is costly and is given for a multitude of purposes. Now we find that it comes on different areas: our being, our belongings and our surroundings. If these areas are critical to the placement of the anointing, then perhaps they will shed some light on the site or sites of the blessing — *there*!

The word *there* has some interesting meanings. Its most understood meaning is "in or at that place."[1] Sometimes it is used in place of a name. For example, you might say to someone, "Hello there." If I take this literally, I can say that if I am operating in the anointing, which comes from unity, then *there* — right on me, Rod Parsley — God will command His blessing.

In another usage *there* expresses emotion. It often is used to show relief, satisfaction or consolation. You might finish a great book, or preach a wonderful message, or eat a delicious meal, then end it by sighing with contentment, "There...." You are relating in only one word that something is finished, and finished with much satisfaction.

After I have preached a message — one which I know has hit the devil where it hurts — I experience a great deal of satisfaction. I can just stomp my foot and say, "There!" To the devil, this one word means, "Your time is up! Your hold is broken! So take that, devil!"

I have heard a mother quiet her crying baby by simply repeating a couple of times, "There, there." That word has a soothing effect. The infant senses relief just in knowing someone listened and cared.

The Head

As Christ is the Head of the Church, everything that comes to us comes from Him. He is the beginning of all things. When the word *head* is used, it refers to the top of anything. Being so prominent, it is usually the most vulnerable part of the body.

And the Lord shall make thee the head, and not the tail; and thou shalt be above only, and thou shalt not be beneath; if that thou hearken unto the commandments of the Lord thy God, which I command thee this day, to observe and to do them.

Deuteronomy 28:13

What is God saying to His people in this passage?

I believe He is speaking directly about the capabilities for leadership that He has placed in each of us. The head houses the brain, which is the center of all our thought processes. It is the incubator of ideas.

If the anointing and the blessing are placed *there*, then productive, prosperity-producing thoughts should flow. As your mind is anointed and blessed, your thoughts will be for good and not for evil. Creative and unique ideas for ministry will spring forth.

Money-making ideas and problem-solving answers will come into the head. Paul said, **Let this mind be in you, which was also in Christ Jesus** (Phil. 2:5). He was telling us that all the secrets of the universe are within our grasp.

Inventor, retired businessman, and Charismatic author/teacher Harold Hill wrote an inspiring book several years ago. It relates a powerful truth that is timeless. In *How To Live Like a King's Kid*, Hill gives several accounts of how the blessing of God anointed his mind.[2]

In one such instance, a new power station for which his company had provided the equipment was scheduled to go into operation in four hours. After working with technicians from General Electric, the station's own engineers could not get it to function.

Hundreds of thousands of dollars were on the line, and with only four hours to go they called Harold Hill. As he began to pray, immediately he "knew exactly what was wrong." He saw it as clearly as if he were watching a picture on a TV screen.

When Hill walked into the station, he went right to the spot that was the source of trouble. But as he instructed the technicians in the repair process, they told him they had already checked out everything in that particular piece of equipment. After some discussion they did as they were directed, even though it seemed absurd to them. They had already tried everything. But when they switched it on, it worked perfectly.

Harold Hill had never been in that plant before. The best minds already on the job had not been able to solve the problem. They knew the equipment and had been dealing with the problem night and day. Harold Hill was only an outside consultant, but he carried inside him the invisible force of the Holy Spirit. The best minds cannot compete with a blessed mind!

In the Bible we see how David took the head of Goliath. (1 Sam. 17:54.) That giant was thirteen feet four inches tall and was covered in armor, but he was threatening only as long he had his head. David was aware that if he took the head he conquered all.

David knew God would protect his head in the day of battle. (Ps. 140:7.) No matter what he faced, his head was anointed. (Ps. 23:5.) The Almighty God was the glory and the lifter of his head. (Ps. 3:3.)

In the New Testament we see how John the Baptist would not be silenced. He spoke directly to Herod about his sin. Imprisonment did not stop his attack on the sin of Herod and Herodias. The only way Herod could silence him was to take his head. (Mark 6:16-29.)

Ephesians 6:17, in describing the armor of God, reminds us to put on the helmet of salvation. It is most important that the head be covered. Most sin begins in the mind, and the mind controls the actions. It is *there* that we need to be covered and anointed. It is *there* that we receive the blessing of God.

Paul admonished, **Be renewed in the spirit of your mind** (Eph. 4:23). He must have known that there was fresh dew, fresh anointing available daily. We can receive a new anointing and blessings each day *there* as we renew our minds. When the Church becomes of one mind, it will live in peace (2 Cor. 13:11), and *there* God will command His blessing.

The Beard

In the writings of the Old Testament, long beards are mentioned in relationship to only five men. In addition to Aaron's beard, the Scripture mentions specifically long beards worn by Samson, David, David's men and the prophet Ezekiel.[3]

The culture of that time period may have made a difference in the importance or the appearance of beards. In ancient cultures the presence of a beard had significance. The Egyptians wore false beards. Beards were braided and styled in a length indicating rank.

The beard was sometimes regarded as a sign of manhood. It gave a man a certain standing with people. He was considered to have matured and, therefore, was worthy of respect.

When we reach maturity in Christ, we receive the fullness of the blessing. Often the growth process is painful. Many times we fail.

You may operate in the anointing and see the hand of God move through you. You may operate in all the gifts and be highly sought after for your ministry. If you have not grown up in the things of God, however, you will not receive the blessing.

In his letters to the churches, Paul spoke regarding the fivefold ministry. He told the church at Ephesus why the ministry offices were given: in preparation for unity. This unity then brings us to maturity so we will be in a position to receive the fullness of the blessing of God.

To prepare God's people for works of service, so that the body of Christ may be built up until we all reach unity in the faith and in the knowledge of the Son of God and become mature, attaining to the whole measure of the fullness of Christ.

Ephesians 4:12,13 NIV

The blessing comes on that maturity as we are working together in one accord. When the Church members begin to work together, each member will experience the blessing of God. Each part will come to know the fullness of God as it joins with the other parts, and they all join together in the work.

In ancient times the beard was often worn for ornamental purposes.[4] It was a personal decoration worn with pride as one would wear jewelry. An ornament is a showpiece, something that enhances natural beauty; it usually catches the eye, drawing attention to whatever it decorates.

We are serving a God Who splashed colors in a rainbow across the sky to remind us of a promise. (Gen. 9:12,13.) That same God accented the earth with a variety of flowers and plants. By speaking a word He created unique and colorful living things in the sea, in the air and on the earth.

Obviously we worship a God Who enjoys unique, colorful and beautiful things. He longs to beautify us. He desires that we stand out in a crowd and display His glory. When God blesses us, He is showing us off.

The enemy cringes when one of God's beloved is noticed because of a blessing. He seeks to steal everything from the beloved so that the blessing will never be seen. When God blesses His children, they stand out. People recognize something special *there*, and they want to know the secret.

Also, in ancient cultures the beard was considered a mark of distinction. Often only the free man could wear a beard; slaves were clean shaven. A man with a beard was the head of his home. He was free to come and go as he pleased, and was in control of his own destiny.

There — in freedom — you find the blessing of God. When you have been released from the chains of sin's bondage you are set free. You are free to receive every promise and blessing of God. You are free to operate in the anointing that is available to you. You wear your freedom like an ornament.

When a medal is given in honor of some great achievement, it is often referred to as a decoration. People can see when you — the blessed one — have been decorated by God. They recognize the blessing and honor God has placed on your life. Your decoration, your ornamentation, is a sign to the world that *there* — on you — God has commanded His blessing.

Loss of a beard in Scripture often was a sign of mourning.[5] Without the anointing, no real blessing of God ever manifests itself. It is the anointing that breaks every yoke of bondage. When deliverance comes, God is then able to open the windows of heaven and rain down blessings on His anointed ones...*there.*

The Garments

And, behold, a woman, which was diseased with an issue of blood twelve years, came behind him and touched the hem of his garment:

For she said within herself, If I may but touch his garment, I shall be whole.

Matthew 9:20,21

The same anointing that was on Jesus also covered His garments. Any blessing from the Father that came through Jesus operating in the anointing permeated the very fabric of the clothing He was wearing. The garment was His covering. He was anointed and covered by the fullness of God.

When we have received the anointing, we should be operating in that fullness of God. Then from our overflow, everything we touch and everything touching us should be blessed.

In the Old Testament we saw how the anointing flowed through the mantle, or garment as well. Elisha had watched Elijah operate in the anointing. He had seen the blessing of God on the ministry of that prophet, and he longed for that same anointing. As a matter of fact, he wanted twice the amount Elijah had. Elijah's mantle was the means God used to pass the anointing from one man to another. (1 Kings 19:19.)

Elijah and Elisha ministered in uniquely different ways, but the anointing and blessing on their lives and ministries were from the same Source. God had commanded His blessing *there* on Elijah and it had affected even his cloak.

The mantle was a garment of covering. Many references are made in the New Testament to the power of God flowing through garments. As we have read in Matthew's gospel, the woman with the issue of blood believed if she could only touch the hem of Jesus' garment she would be healed.

Others sought to touch the hem of His garment and, as Matthew 14:36 says, **...as many as touched were made perfectly whole.** As the overflow of the anointing permeated even His garments, that healing virtue went forth when people came in contact with His clothing.

The same anointing occurred in the apostle Paul:

> **And God wrought special miracles by the hands of Paul:**
>
> **So that from his body were brought unto the sick handkerchiefs or aprons, and the disease departed from them, and the evil spirits went out of them.**
>
> **Acts 19:11,12**

Paul was used by God to perform many miracles. Historical records bear out that, even though Paul was an eloquent speaker, people were drawn to his ministry because of the power of God emanating from him.

God saw in Paul a surrendered vessel that could be used to do remarkable things for the kingdom. Because Paul was submitted to the will of God for his life, God was able to perform those special miracles through him.

The anointing was so evident in Paul's life that *handkerchiefs and aprons* which had been in contact with his body carried his anointing. Some translations of this Scripture list the pieces as scarves, towels or clothing. Whatever the pieces of material, the anointing of God flowed through them to the needy ones. When the people received their miracle they were touched with a blessing from God.

Keep Your Garments White

We need to get to the place where the blessing of God is so evident in our lives that even our garments reflect it.

Many have operated in the anointing and miracles have occurred. Few, however, have been so full of the anointing in their own lives that the blessing of God just flowed from them onto their garments.

> **Let thy garments be always white; and let thy head lack no ointment.**
>
> **Ecclesiastes 9:8**

Perhaps the blessing has been missing because we have failed to keep our garments white. The anointing has been made available to us. The anointing has been given, yet many continue to fail God in their own personal lives. The Church has fallen so short of all God has ordained it to be.

It is time that we be washed again in the precious blood of the Lamb. It is time for us to cleanse ourselves again by the washing of the water of the Word. (Eph. 5:26.) It is time to purify. It is time to place our filthy garments on the altar of sacrifice.

If you really desire to see the blessing of God, everything that has contaminated and condemned must go. It is time for the world to see God's blessing on everything with which we come in contact. When we are walking in truth and living in unity, our garments will be kept white and we will experience the fullness of the blessing of God.

> **I will greatly rejoice in the Lord, my soul shall be joyful in my God; for he hath clothed me with the garments of salvation, he hath covered me with the robe of righteousness, as a bridegroom decketh himself with ornaments, and as a bride adorneth herself with her jewels.**
>
> **Isaiah 61:10**

Zion

Old Testament Zion is generally recognized as a specific place. But there has been some confusion in understanding Zion. Several Scripture verses offer different perspectives. Let's look at some of them:

> **Nevertheless David took the strong hold of Zion: the same is the city of David.**
>
> **2 Samuel 5:7**

> **Then the moon shall be confounded, and the sun ashamed, when the Lord of hosts shall reign in mount Zion, and in Jerusalem, and before his ancients gloriously.**
>
> **Isaiah 24:23**

> **And I will make her that halted a remnant, and her that was cast far off a strong nation: and the Lord shall reign over them in mount Zion from henceforth, even for ever.**
>
> **Micah 4:7**

> **I bring near my righteousness; it shall not be far off, and my salvation shall not tarry: and I will place salvation in Zion for Israel my glory.**
>
> **Isaiah 46:13**

We can take the word *Zion* to mean both an actual place and a place with a figurative meaning. David often referred to *Zion* as an object of God's honor or punishment, His children. From the Old Testament Hebrew translation the root meaning of *Zion* is "parched place."[6] That's a barren and dry place, a wilderness. In the New Testament the spelling is sometimes changed from *Zion* to *Sion*, and its Greek definition is "the Church."[7]

It may seem like the Church is dead and dry, but we are His Bride. We have been chosen and set apart. We have been given the gift of eternal life. He has already paid a great price for us. He left His Holy Spirit with us to live in us and empower us — to revive the dead, dry bones of the Church.

The anointing was given so the Church would be moisturized. We can receive His anointing. Above all, He longs to bless us. Much is available to us. We must operate within the guidance of His Word. He is not coming back for a brittle, wrinkled-up Bride.

When we serve Him with our whole being and worship Him in spirit and in truth, we will be in unity.

You may be experiencing the greatest drought of your life, but your need can be supplied. That anointing is like the dew on Mount Hermon and on the mountains of Zion. It doesn't matter how bad the drought gets on Mount Zion and on Mount Hermon. There is always dew like a gully-washing rain from the night before.

It doesn't matter if it looks like your need is not going to be supplied. It doesn't matter if the doctor looks at you and says that you can't live but have to die. It doesn't matter if you are in the winter of your life. You may think there is no way you can bear fruit because your parched, dry soul cannot take it a moment longer.

If that is you, my friend, begin to seek God for the anointing. Your darkest hour will soon be like the glistening radiance of the noonday sun. God will water your parched land!

You can't stop the dew; it is new every morning. So hold on. Weeping only lasts through the night; joy comes in the morning. (Ps. 30:5.) It may look dark when you go to bed, but just turn over and pillow your head in the presence of God. Then the next morning everything will be all right.

Get to the house of the Lord. You will see your brothers there. You will see your sisters there. They will pray with you there. They will believe with you there, and that anointing will be like the dew of Hermon and Zion. *There* He will command His blessing!

[1]*Webster's New Collegiate Dictionary* (Springfield, MA: Merriam-Webster, 1979).

[2]Harold Hill, *How to Live Like a King's Kid* (Plainfield, NJ: Logos, 1974), pp. 157-159.

[3]Finis J. Dake, *Dake's Annotated Reference Bible* (Lawrenceville, GA: Dake Bibles, 1976), p. 611.

[4]*Smith's Bible Dictionary* (Nashville: Thomas Nelson), p. 34.

[5]Ibid.

[6]J. B. Jackson, *A Dictionary of the Proper Names of the Old and New Testament Scriptures* (Neptune, NJ: Loizeaux Bros., 1957), p. 99.

[7]James Strong, *Strong's Exhaustive Concordance*, (Iowa Falls: World Bible Publ.), "Greek Dictionary of the New Testament," p. 65, #4622.

PART 4 — The Commanded Blessing

9

The Command Effect

And God said...and it was so.

Genesis 1

There is a television commercial that has always intrigued me. The scene is a crowded room with people noisily chattering. One gentleman leans over to another and says, "My broker is E. F. Hutton, and he says...." Immediately the room is silent. All those standing around stop dead in their tracks, straining to hear what E. F. Hutton said. Then the announcer firmly states, "When E. F. Hutton speaks, everybody listens."

As clever as this advertising technique is, I couldn't help but wonder what type of man could command such intense interest in his words. As pastor of a large congregation I thought it would help me tremendously to know his secret.

We were not dealing in such different markets. That broker was talking investments with high-paying dividends; I was talking investments with rewards that would last through eternity.

In those ads, his words captured the attention of everyone within earshot. People in a busy restaurant stopped eating to feast on what he was saying. Dancers stopped in midair and the Bolshoi Ballet came to a screeching halt when one person in the audience only whispered the name, E. F. Hutton.

I wanted to know what kind of man could command so much attention with his words. I needed this information for when I preached on Sunday mornings. Like that man, I was declaring to my congregation, "My God is an awesome God, *and my God says....*"

I wanted the yawning, snoozing, doodling, Life Saver-munching, bubble gum-poppin' saints to stop what they were doing. I wanted them to hear every word God was going to use me to speak to them, because my God has something worth hearing to say!

When God commanded the attention of the elements of the earth He had no problem being heard. The winds and the waves obeyed Him. When He began to address His commands to humans, however, He encountered a problem known as selective hearing loss. (We will consider that problem later in this chapter.)

Throughout the Word we find the commands of God time and time again. God's Word is still the ultimate challenge. It is always truth given for the good of mankind.

Before the end of time, everything He has promised will come to pass. As a matter of fact, He guards His Word. He will perform all He has promised. (Luke 1:45.)

When God speaks, His Word goes forth to declare, teach, challenge, subdue and direct. In each instance His Word is backed by power and an uncompromised truth. When God speaks, everyone *should* listen — including E. F. Hutton!

> **He that hath an ear, let him hear what the Spirit saith unto the churches.**
>
> **Revelation 3:6**

God Commanded, Response Demanded

In the beginning when God spoke, all nature responded to His command. Ten times in the first chapter of Genesis, we see how *God said*, and there was an immediate response. Even as God uttered the words, the creative processes had already occurred.

When God spoke, darkness responded. It had to dissipate at the sound of His voice.

God spoke to the wide-open spaces and to the waters, and they parted at His direction. He spoke to the dry land exposed, and it did as it was told: it brought forth vegetation. He spoke into existence the sun, the moon and stars in the heavens.

God once again commanded the waters and they brought forth life. When He spoke to the firmament, it too brought forth life. God was so pleased with the results of the Word He had commanded that He blessed it. When He spoke again to the earth, it responded with life — and He blessed it.

He then spoke His desire to make man. When that process was completed He blessed it, both male and female. Then He gave them a command: that they be fruitful and multiply. He told Adam and Eve what to eat; but, most importantly, He told them what not to eat. He gave man the direction, then followed it with the penalty for disobedience to His command.

Adam and Eve, and all born after them, developed selective hearing loss. The human race was given freedom of choice, and we frequently exercise that right by refusing to listen to the commanded Word of God.

> **And God said unto Noah, The end of all flesh is come before Me; for the earth is filled with violence through them; and, behold, I will destroy them with the earth.**
>
> **Make thee an ark....**
>
> **Genesis 6:13,14**

God spoke to Noah and told him to build a boat. His instructions were explicit, detailed in every way.

In spite of harassment by those around him, Noah obeyed God, and he and his family were saved from the flood. When God spoke, Noah listened!

> **Thus did Noah; according to all that God commanded him, so did he.**
>
> **Genesis 6:22**

The most recognizable of all God's commands are those dictated to Moses. They were to be given as directives for God's people to serve as the basic rules of life. These guidelines were not the ten suggestions, they were the Ten Commandments:

> **And God spake all these words, saying,**
>
> **I am the Lord thy God, which have brought thee out of the land of Egypt, out of the house of bondage.**
>
> **Thou shalt have no other gods before me.**
>
> **Thou shalt not make unto thee any graven image, or any likeness of any thing that is in heaven above, or that is in the earth beneath, or that is in the water under the earth:**
>
> **Thou shalt not bow down thyself to them, nor serve them: for I the Lord thy God am a jealous God, visiting the iniquity of the fathers upon the children unto the third and fourth generation of them that hate me;**
>
> **And shewing mercy unto thousands of them that love me, and keep my commandments.**

Thou shalt not take the name of the Lord thy God in vain; for the Lord will not hold him guiltless that taketh his name in vain.

Remember the sabbath day, to keep it holy.

Six days shalt thou labour, and do all thy work:

But the seventh day is the sabbath of the Lord thy God: in it thou shalt not do any work, thou, nor thy son, nor thy daughter, thy manservant, nor thy maidservant, nor thy cattle, nor thy stranger that is within thy gates:

For in six days the Lord made heaven and earth, the sea, and all that in them is, and rested the seventh day: wherefore the Lord blessed the sabbath day, and hallowed it.

Honour thy father and thy mother: that thy days may be long upon the land which the Lord thy God giveth thee.

Thou shalt not kill.

Thou shalt not commit adultery.

Thou shalt not steal.

Thou shalt not bear false witness against thy neighbour.

Thou shalt not covet thy neighbour's house, thou shalt not covet thy neighbour's wife, nor his manservant, nor his maidservant, nor his ox, nor his ass, nor any thing that is thy neighbour's.

Exodus 20:1-17

The commanded Word of God brought with it a promise. If the directives were obeyed they would bring life. God also promised that He would prolong our days upon the earth in the land we would possess if His commandments were kept. (Deut. 5:33.)

Strength and prosperity were promised for obedience to God's commanded Word. Mercy was given as a benefit. Increase and the promise for things to go well with our children are also given.

Be Strong

God spoke to Joshua and commanded him to be strong. Now this is a command that seems to be easier said than done. When God says, *Be strong*, you must be strong. Three times in the first chapter of the book of Joshua, God spoke to him to be strong.

God followed up His commandment with a promise that made the order easier to bear. He told Joshua that He would be with him wherever he went. Further He said, **This book of the law shall not depart out of thy mouth; but thou shalt meditate therein day and night, that thou mayest observe to do according to all that is written therein: for then thou shalt make thy way prosperous, and then thou shalt have good success** (Josh. 1:8).

Now everyone enjoys a good promise of success and prosperity. Many balk, however, at God's command to be strong. People would rather do a million other things than meditate on the Word of God day and night.

If you are not fortified with God's Word, you will not be able to obey His commands. If you are not grounded in God's Word, when the winds of adversity blow, you will not be able to stand. If you are not rooted deeply in the truth of His Word, you will be tossed when the storms of life come.

David said that the righteous — those in right standing with God — would flourish like the palm tree. (Ps. 92:12.) We must be firmly rooted in the things of God. For us to be strong when the trials come, we will have to know the truths of God's Word. For us to survive, that Word will have to be imbedded in us.

This is what the Lord says:

Cursed is the one who trusts in man, who depends on flesh for his strength and whose heart turns away from the Lord.

He will be like a bush in the wastelands; he will not see prosperity when it comes.

He will dwell in the parched places of the desert, in a salt land where no one lives.

But blessed is the man who trusts in the Lord, whose confidence is in him.

He will be like a tree planted by the water that sends out its roots by the stream.

It does not fear when heat comes; its leaves are always green.

It has no worries in a year of drought and never fails to bear fruit.

Jeremiah 17:5-8 NIV

If you are rooted, grounded and founded in God's Word, you will be obedient to His commands. You will recognize His voice when He speaks. You will stand when your faith is tested because you will know the Truth. You will not be deceived by the winds of unsound doctrine. You will be strong.

Doubting God

Gideon saw himself as a weakling, but God sent an angel to declare His Word to him. Fearful of the Midianites, Gideon had been threshing wheat by the winepress to hide it. (Judg. 6:11.) The angel addressed Gideon as **mighty man of valour** (v. 12). God saw Gideon in a way that he did not see himself — strong.

And the Lord looked upon him, and said, Go in this thy might, and thou shalt save Israel from the hand of the Midianites: have not I sent thee?

Judges 6:14

God commanded Gideon to go. His promise to him was that He would be with him. Gideon reminded God that he was a nothing; maybe God had forgotten that he was the least in his father's house. (v. 15.) But God promised Gideon again that He would be with him. He had God's Word on the fact that they would be victorious.

Still, Gideon was hesitant to obey the commanded Word of God. He was not sure if his ears were hearing correctly. He had to put out a fleece to ensure that the Word was really from God. He needed assurance that God would be with him and give them the victory as promised.

Oh, how this is like the Church today! Reading the Word, hearing the Word, singing the Word, even living much of the Word. Yet when the Lord speaks, they doubt. God is telling the Church today to grow up and get into unity. He is calling on us to live all we have been taught.

God is demanding that the Church live in complete holiness. Yet many in the Church doubt that this is the voice of God they are hearing. Like Gideon, the Church has tested again and again to see if this is really God's voice. The Body of Christ has had difficulty in accepting that God is speaking — commanding — us to come into unity.

Selective Hearing Loss

The Church has been selective in what it wants to hear. Much of the truth of God's Word has been hard to take. It has seemed too difficult to live holy, too difficult to tithe.

People have listened when the Word suited their own personal, pet religious ideas. When the Word started touching their own areas of weakness they suddenly developed a hearing problem. They thought, surely God was not speaking to them.

People have become selective in regard to those with whom they wish to worship. The Church has felt that it has the right to segregate itself. Self-righteous "country clubs" have been built with the name of a church placed over the door. But it is time that we get into unity. It is the commanded Word of God.

Specific directions came from God, through an angel, to a man named Manoah and his barren wife. The promise was given that a child would be born to her. But certain commands were to be followed. (Judg. 13.) God was very precise in this directive. The wife was told in detail what she could not eat or drink, and they both were given some specific instructions as to their child's upbringing.

Samson was that child of promise. When grown, he was used by God to wreak havoc among the Philistines, the enemies of God's chosen people.

And the people murmured against Moses, saying, What shall we drink?

And he cried unto the Lord; and the Lord shewed him a tree, which when he had cast into the waters, the waters were made sweet: there he made for them a statute and an ordinance, and there he proved them,

And said, If thou wilt diligently hearken to the voice of the Lord thy God, and wilt do that which is right in his sight, and wilt give ear to his commandments, and keep all his statutes, I will put none of these diseases upon thee, which I have brought upon the Egyptians: for I am the Lord that healeth thee.

Exodus 15:24-26

God still has commandments for eating habits today, but many just refuse to listen. They would rather spend money exercising off their excesses. At the same time they close their ears to the basic principles of healthy eating that God gave to His children in the Levitical laws.

David begged the Lord to hear his voice; he wanted God's ears to be attentive to his cries and his needs. (Ps. 130:2.) Today, people expect God to listen to them and respond every time they speak, but when God speaks, that's a different story.

The Word Made Flesh

And the Word was made flesh, and dwelt among us, (and we beheld his glory, the glory as of the only begotten of the Father,) full of grace and truth.

John 1:14

When Jesus came, He was the commanded Word of God. All truth was in Him. From the beginning the Word existed with God and the Word was God. (John 1:1.) Whenever Jesus spoke, He spoke the very Word of God.

Jesus answered and said unto him, If a man love me, he will keep my words: and my Father will love him, and we will come unto him, and make our abode with him.

He that loveth me not keepeth not my sayings: and the word which ye hear is not mine, but the Father's which sent me.

John 14:23,24

A Mother's Wisdom

Mary, the mother of Jesus, knew the power that was resident within Him. Before He operated in the fullness of His miracle-working power, she was aware of His capabilities. Perhaps she was over-zealous in her attempt to see Him operate in the fullness of His call.

During a wedding feast, a crisis arose when the host ran out of wine. Mary probably discreetly whispered in Jesus' ear, "They have no more wine." He knew His mother's words meant much more than they were saying.

We have no way of knowing what He was thinking at the time, but His reply was, **Woman, what have I to do with thee? mine hour is not yet come** (John 2:4). Without further debate the mother ignored what may have been a little jab at her pushy behavior and went to the servants.

> **His mother saith unto the servants, Whatsoever he saith unto you, do it.**
>
> **John 2:5**

Mary knew that whatever He commanded would come to pass. She was confident in the Word she was given at His conception. She had quietly carried that Word. She had pondered it in her heart all those years and longed to see the fulfillment of what she had been told.

Jesus began by commanding the servants, and then the water turned to wine.

Another time He spoke to the dead daughter of a synagogue ruler. He took her by the hand and commanded her to arise, and she did. (Mark 5:35-42.)

He commanded the multitude to sit so He could feed them. They ate and were filled. (Mark 6:39-42.)

Many times He commanded unclean spirits to come out of those possessed — and they did!

He even commanded the winds and the waves to be still — and they were! (Mark 4:39.)

Whenever the Lord speaks, there will be a response. You may choose not to listen. You may choose not to answer. If you ignore His voice, that is your response. You might even listen but then refuse to obey. He is always speaking, and we are always choosing. When we hear, will we obey?

Every word Jesus spoke was from the heart of God. Each time He spoke, the Word brought life. His Word is spirit food, nourishing those who listen and obey.

In Deuteronomy 8:3 and again in Matthew 4:4 we read, ...**Man shall not live by bread alone, but by every word that proceedeth out of the mouth of God.** In God's commandments there is life, there is health, and there is freedom.

It is not enough that we feed our physical bodies. We need spiritual food, and that can only be found in the Word of God.

The Church is full of malnourished Christians. On Sunday morning they are hungry enough to park and go in. On Sunday night they only want the drive-through window. By midweek, though famished, they are just too busy with life to feed at the table with God's family.

In the natural, when you fail to feed your body it will eventually shut down. You don't think clearly. You feel weak and weary. Something inside you needs fuel to go on. Even if you are just too busy for a complete meal, you still find a way to eat something.

If you don't eat, you might pass out. If you cannot function on your job, you may lose it. If you cannot drive without going to sleep at the wheel, you could lose your life. If you don't get some food fast, your name will be on a tombstone, and that's not the way you want to be remembered.

When the devil comes around with temptation to sin, that spirit man is a weakling. He hasn't fed on the Word for some time. He hasn't been fortified by the commanded Word to withstand an attack from the devil. He has no strength to resist the tricks of the enemy. There is no spiritual muscle to apply the Word that once burned in his heart. It has been too long since he was nourished by that Word.

What Are You Hungry For?

I don't believe the Church has lost its appetite, but the appetites have changed. We are sophisticated now. No longer do the saints tarry all night until they are filled up. People have forgotten how to wait in the presence of the Lord while He prepares and serves up exactly what their souls are longing for.

The Church has become "hype hungry." The people want to be entertained. They want to laugh and be refreshed. They want to hear a gospel that fits their lifestyle: a quick-fix Christianity. They long to hear a word that will lift them up and sustain them for the rest of the week.

Oh, the Church is hungry alright, but what is it hungry for? Has the Body of Christ lost its taste for the meat of the Word?

Many Christians still want to be spiritual babies that need everything done for them. They want to be bottle fed and have the pastor change their diaper. They want someone to slap oil on their forehead and knock them out under the power, so they can stand up changed. Most of these babies can't digest a full meal of the richness of the Word.

But the Church of the living God is no longer in its infancy. Did you ever notice how quickly babies grow? They just don't stay babies very long. They are always learning new things, needing more food, and outgrowing clothes faster than you can replace them. In spite of the fact that we want them to stay babies a little longer, they grow.

As a baby grows, he needs more nourishment. As the body begins to strengthen, new demands are placed on him. As the child explores new territory, new boundaries must be learned. He hears no a lot.

It is the same in the spirit realm. You can only stay a baby for so long. You must begin to grow and learn the laws governing your spiritual walk. You must learn the boundaries and the limits. You learn these things from the commandments of God.

When a mother loudly says *No!* or slaps her baby's hand as it reaches for a hot oven, she is protecting her child. When God gave the commandments to His children, He was doing the same thing. The commandments of God were given for our protection.

Much like a baby, we don't want to play by the rules. We try again and again to test the limits of authority until we learn what is best for us. Many in the Church have just refused to grow up and assume the responsibilities of a mature Christian.

We have the privileges that maturing brings, but we don't want the responsibility that goes along with it. Many still want to be cared for as if they were babies, but they expect all the privileges belonging to adults.

It is time for the Church to grow up. It is time that we take on the responsibilities of spiritual maturity. It is time to eat and digest the meat of the Word so that our spirit man can be fully developed in the things of God.

Check your spiritual appetite:

When was the last time you wept when you read the Word?

When did the Word last pierce your heart with conviction?

When did you last decide to make a step forward in your spiritual maturity?

How long has it been since you just couldn't wait to spend time reading the Word?

Have you waited in the presence of the Lord lately?

Have you been so determined to get closer to God that you would risk everything just to hear Him speak?

If you really long to do exploits for the kingdom of God, then you have to build some spiritual muscle. Put in some early mornings and late nights in the gymnasium of faith. You will have to sweat a little, groan a little, and persevere.

No one is going to open your Bible for you and put it in your lap. No one is going to wrap you in a blanket and carry you to church. No one will be around to put that praise and worship tape in your cassette player when you are beginning to doubt.

You have to want God and want Him so badly that nothing will stand in the way of your time with His Word. You may need a miracle, but that's not enough reason to seek Him. Do you really want Him? Do you want Him enough to listen to His every Word and obey His every command?

If ye love me, keep my commandments.

John 14:15

What Is Your Love Quotient?

Here we may find the root of the problem. Maybe the Church needs to have a checkup. Perhaps there is a severe deficiency in its love level. Maybe what is needed is a good, old-fashioned revival of love.

Most people want revival so they can see miracles. Many come to special services hoping for signs and wonders. How many come because the Lover of their soul is going to show up and they just want to catch a glimpse of Him?

Is your ear lonely to hear His voice?

Does your heart long to obey His Word even when your flesh is pulling you in the opposite direction?

With the enemy pulling you down, how long has it been since you said like Jesus, "It is my meat to do the will of my Father"?

As the Father hath loved me, so have I loved you: continue ye in my love.

If ye keep my commandments, ye shall abide in my love; even as I have kept my Father's commandments, and abide in his love.

> These things have I spoken unto you, that my joy might remain in you, and that your joy might be full.
>
> This is my commandment, That ye love one another, as I have loved you.
>
> Greater love hath no man than this, that a man lay down his life for his friends.
>
> Ye are my friends, if ye do whatsoever I command you.
>
> **John 15:9-14**

Obedience to the commands of God is the purest sign of your love for Him. Everything you are looking for — direction for every situation in your life — can be found in His Word.

You may have read every self-help book you can find, but you still cannot see the light at the end of the tunnel. You can watch every TV talk show dealing with your area of need but find no answer. You might spend thousands of dollars for the privilege of lying on the couch of some doctor whose walls are covered with degrees, yet go away empty.

What you are looking for, the world cannot give. You need a real love transplant. The Donor has been waiting on you since Calvary. He gave you His all. It is time for you to make full use of the new heart He has placed within you. (Ezek. 36:26,27.) You have a greater capacity for love than you know.

You always find the time to do what is most important to you. How do you spend your time? If you told me your schedule for one week, I could easily pinpoint your priorities. God wants you to love Him, abide in Him, and keep His commandments, that your joy might be full.

When the pressures of life are overwhelming, you can bear them. You can be an overcomer. You do not need to hide in drugs or alcohol. Once you become His, you are automatically an overcomer, by His Word.

> **Whosoever believeth that Jesus is the Christ is born of God: and every one that loveth him that begat loveth him also that is begotten of him.**
>
> **By this we know that we love the children of God, when we love God, and keep his commandments.**
>
> **For this is the love of God, that we keep his commandments: and his commandments are not grievous.**
>
> **For whatsoever is born of God overcometh the world: and this is the victory that overcometh the world, even our faith.**
>
> **Who is he that overcometh the world, but he that believeth that Jesus is the Son of God?**
>
> **1 John 5:1-5**

Is it little wonder why the Body is having so much trouble coming into unity? Too many in the Church are unwilling to love God as the Scripture commands. If they are unable to commit themselves to the One Who gave Himself for them, how can they give themselves in love to each other?

The very cornerstone of our faith is love. It is the commanded Word of God. If the Church is ever to be all it is called to be, then it *must* walk in obedience to God's Word — and love one another.

> And now I beseech thee, lady, not as though I wrote a new commandment unto thee, but that which we had from the beginning, that we love one another.
>
> And this is love, that we walk after his commandments. This is the commandment, That, as ye have heard from the beginning, ye should walk in it.
>
> 2 John 5,6

Many churches and denominations have hundreds of pages full of rules and regulations for their members. Often these guidelines are amended, rewritten, rearranged, recommended, confirmed and ratified annually by the governing committees.

Many churches have regulated themselves right out of the power that resides in God's Word. Something has been missing, and we know it. Few are being brave enough to stand boldly before their congregations and command them to do anything — even with the authority of God's Word as their source.

When church members come looking for answers, the elders and deacons rally to formulate opinions. But few have the honesty or humility to say, "I don't have the answer, but I will help you search the Word until we find it, together."

It is time we get back to the most basic truth of all — the Word of God.

Lost Love

When John the Revelator wrote to the church at Ephesus, he first commended them, then rebuked them. Something had been missing in their service to God.

> **I know thy works, and thy labour, and thy patience, and how thou canst not bear them which are evil: and thou hast tried them which say they are apostles, and are not, and hast found them liars:**
>
> **And hast borne, and hast patience, and for my name's sake hast laboured, and hast not fainted.**
>
> **Nevertheless I have somewhat against thee, because thou hast left thy first love.**
>
> **Revelation 2:2-4**

The church at Ephesus had been doing a lot of things right. The believers were working hard. They had been patient in trials and they did not tolerate evil. They had discerned some spirits that were not of God.

In all their trials they endured and did not faint, but that wasn't enough. They had forgotten their first love. They had forgotten the greatest of the commandments.

This church had been functioning during difficult times. It had faced persecution and false teachers, but it seemed to have met each challenge victoriously.

With all the good they had done, still John confronted them. He called them to repentance. They needed to do first things first. They were to remember their first love.

The very One on Whom the New Testament Church was founded had taken second place to plans and programs. The Son of God — Who had given His life because He loved first — was no longer of primary importance to them.

The Church today has become so good at planning. Our programs are the latest and the greatest. The how-tos of ministry are printed in books and magazines. We can preach a perfect message by using someone else's outline of three points and a poem. We can get a video kit on how to build a successful Sunday school program. We can have seminars to learn soulwinning. We can listen to an audio tape and learn the fine art of intercession.

We can spend hours planning and doing the work of the Lord. But have we forgotten the Lord of the work?

Like the children of Israel, God has given the Church what we have wanted, and the price is leanness of soul. But undernourished and lacking the strength to carry on the work, some have lost their first love.

The Church hasn't stopped growing. It hasn't stopped building. It hasn't stopped developing new committees to make new plans. But many churches have forgotten to consult the original builder and maker, the King of kings and Lord of lords.

The Church needs to take a break and remember its first love. Have you asked Jesus about your plans? Possibly He would enjoy a moment or two of your time. Maybe you could postpone a committee meeting and spend some time with Him.

The Spirit of the Lord is wooing His Church, His Bride, back to Himself. He wants to bless us. We are His beloved, and He has many promises that He longs to fulfill in our behalf.

It shouldn't be so difficult to follow His Word. Above all, we must learn to follow the commandment to love. When we listen and obey His voice, the promised blessing will follow.

> **If ye be willing and obedient, ye shall eat the good of the land.**
>
> **Isaiah 1:19**
>
> **Blessed are they that do his commandments....**
>
> **Revelation 22:14**

10
The Overflow

And it shall come to pass, if thou shalt hearken diligently unto the voice of the Lord thy God, to observe and to do all his commandments which I command thee this day, that the Lord thy God will set thee on high above all nations of the earth:

And all these blessings shall come on thee, and overtake thee, if thou shalt hearken unto the voice of the Lord thy God.

Blessed shalt thou be in the city, and blessed shalt thou be in the field.

Blessed shall be the fruit of thy body, and the fruit of thy ground, and the fruit of thy cattle, the increase of thy kine, and the flocks of thy sheep.

Blessed shall be thy basket and thy store.

Blessed shalt thou be when thou comest in, and blessed shalt thou be when thou goest out.

The Lord shall cause thine enemies that rise up against thee to be smitten before thy face: they shall come out against thee one way, and flee before thee seven ways.

The Lord shall command the blessing upon thee in thy storehouses, and in all that thou settest thine hand unto; and he shall bless thee in the land which the Lord thy God giveth thee.

The Lord shall establish thee an holy people unto himself, as he hath sworn unto thee, if thou shalt keep the commandments of the Lord thy God, and walk in his ways.

And all people of the earth shall see that thou art called by the name of the Lord; and they shall be afraid of thee.

And the Lord shall make thee plenteous in goods, in the fruit of thy body, and in the fruit of thy cattle, and in the fruit of thy ground, in the land which the Lord sware unto thy fathers to give thee.

The Lord shall open unto thee his good treasure, the heaven to give the rain unto thy land in his season, and to bless all the work of thine hand: and thou shalt lend unto many nations, and thou shalt not borrow.

And the Lord shall make thee the head, and not the tail; and thou shalt be above only, and thou shalt not be beneath; if that thou hearken unto the commandments of the Lord thy God, which I command thee this day, to observe and to do them:

And thou shalt not go aside from any of the words which I command thee this day, to the right hand, or to the left, to go after other gods to serve them.

Deuteronomy 28:1-14

Every possible blessing is available to the believer today. God has provided through His promises everything you could possibly want or need. All these wonderful things are yours, with just a few important conditions.

You must listen intently for the voice of God. Often He speaks in that still, small voice, so you must always be listening. You do not want to miss anything God may be whispering to you.

Dominated by the Doctrines of the Faith

The commandments must become a part of your daily living. They are your God-directed guidelines for health, happiness and holiness. They will keep you from much harm if you allow your life to be dominated by their precepts.

You have seen the nature and character of Jesus through the recorded Word of God. Now walk in His ways. You are to become an imitator of God, the mirror image of Him. When you walk like Him you will reflect His likeness. As you take on more of His character, when others look at you, all they will see is Jesus.

You are not to turn aside from any of the commands of God. There is no excuse for watering down or creating your own interpretation of His commandments. When you have come to know His heart, you will realize the eternal importance of His commanded Word.

What Do You Worship?

You are not to go after other gods and serve them. More than any other temptation this is the greatest threat to the Church. This commandment is broken every day of the week, and the Church has not even realized it has transgressed the law of God.

You may not have built an idol of wood or stone. You probably have not erected a shrine in your back yard. But what about that one sitting in your family room with antennae horns and an electric cord tail?

It may be difficult for you to shout unto God with a voice of triumph when your pastor directs you to do so. But hour after hour you can make yourself hoarse by reacting to a game you are watching on TV. Whenever your favorite team scores a touchdown or makes a basket, you leap from your recliner, whooping in joy.

You will spend hours, if necessary, on your job — worshiping the almighty dollar — just so you can own the biggest and best of everything. You will set aside plenty of time for your expensive and time-consuming hobby god. You will diligently strive to become the best on the golf course, the tennis court or wherever your passion may be, regardless of the time or money you must invest.

You will worship at the shrine of your god, *Self*. You will spend hours and every extra penny on improving yourself. The health club, the plastic surgeon's office, the cosmetic counters and the clothing stores are your places of worship.

Sadly, when God is replaced, the "other gods" are many. During the summer you worship the lawn or the lake. In the fall you worship football. You will allow something — anything — to rob your time and attention from God.

But God is a jealous God. He is not going to share our devotion. What is it going to take for the Church to stop worshiping other gods? When will the Church realize that the only way to receive all God has promised is to honor His Word — all of His Word?

I Want the Blessings

It is time we started receiving all God has promised. I am tired of living with less than God's best. I am tired of wondering just what it takes to move the hand of God. Now I know the key: obedience. With the key of obedience as my companion I can unlock the goodness of God. The riches of heaven are at my disposal.

Deuteronomy 28 lists 21 blessings. I want all of them — and the ones in Deuteronomy, chapter 11, too (we will look at them later). I want everything God has made available to me. I am His child and these promises are for His children.

Walking in obedience, you can expect to be set high above all the nations of the earth. When you obey, others will see and look up to you because you operate in wisdom and strength through the power of God. Your life will be an example to the world. You will be a reflection of the light and the glory of God.

You can expect to be blessed in the city. You will be blessed in the countryside. Wherever you work, wherever you play, you will find the blessing of God covering you there. It is His promise. It is His direct response to your obedience.

Obedient followers of God are promised perfect children. In this day and age that is a promise worth holding on to. If you follow the voice of God, you will receive specific direction in the upbringing of your children. You will have discernment and will recognize trouble before it reaches them. You will rely on Holy Ghost power to come against the enemy — every sickness, every disabling force — that would set itself up against your children.

You will speak to your children with wisdom, and they will respond. They will recognize the Source of your wisdom and will see His wisdom reflected in your life.

The labors of your hands will be blessed of God. The places where you have tilled, planted and watered will receive His blessing. As you plant according to His Word, you will discover that He knows the perfect season and the most fertile soil. At His direction your crops will be blessed.

Unless you are a rancher, God's promise of increase to your cattle and flocks is probably never taken seriously. You wouldn't know what to do with a cow if you had one. You don't wear wool and you never eat lamb, so why would you want to own a flock of sheep?

In the days of Moses, prosperity was measured by the number of cattle and sheep you possessed. Owning large herds and flocks meant you would never be hungry or want for clothing. You always had wool and hides for making garments. If your flocks and herds were great in number, you would have many herdsmen. You would employ enough to simply care for all you possessed.

Your baskets and your storehouses will be full. When you obey God you will be so blessed that everything you have will be running over with His goodness. There will be no emptiness left unfilled.

There will be so much of the good things God has given. Whenever and wherever there is a need for the Word of God, there will be plenty to draw from in the storehouse. The provision will be there to take the richness and the goodness of God to the nations. From the overflow of your blessings, God's Word will go forth.

Everything you undertake will be blessed. What a promise! This will happen because you are listening clearly to the direction of God and you will not undertake foolish projects.

You will have the mind of Christ, and whatever He tells you to do will be blessed. It will not be your idea or your project that is blessed, but the projects given and directed by God as you have responded to His leading.

You will have complete victory over your enemies. You will not be fighting in your own strength. You will arm yourself with the wisdom and might that comes from God. You will be empowered to outwit every force that comes against you. You are covered, armed and strengthened by the power of His might, and no foe will be able to stand against you.

Your land will be fertile and productive. You will not waste valuable time and money in areas that will not give you the greatest return. You are God's child and, as you walk in obedience to His Word, you will have the best.

When people look at you they will recognize the blessing of God on your life. They will see your holiness as you walk according to all the commands God has given. You will be established in righteousness and your brightness will shine as the noonday sun.

You will be so full of the goodness of God that you will testify and stand as a witness to all He has done. Your life will be a glorious example to the world that you are blessed by God. Your bold witness will bring others to know and to be partakers in all that is of God.

There will be an awesome respect for who you are and Whom you serve. The ungodly will fear coming against you because you operate in the mighty power of the Most High.

Again, Deuteronomy 28 reminds us that the blessing of God brings prosperity in every area of your life. You will be rich in goods, children, stock and crops. You will have more than enough of everything God has to offer.

The Lord will open all His good treasure and will bring revelation to you. You will come to intimately know His nature. You will not be moved by the forces of darkness or by the dictates of your flesh. You will be so in tune with the voice of God that you will be directed and motivated by His good pleasure.

You will receive such favor from God that even the skies will open to the refreshing you need. Your crops will receive all that is necessary as the Lord directs the seasons. You will never need to experience crop failure if you are walking in obedience to His Word.

When you are obedient, everything you set your hand to will be successful. You will never have to be a failure at anything again. You can have all of heaven backing you up — you just have to obey.

You will be so prosperous that you will have money to lend to others who are less fortunate than you. You will be asking your banker how you can help them. You will never again need credit cards. You don't need *MasterCard* — you just need the Master!

David said in Psalm 35:27 that the Lord takes pleasure in the prosperity of His servants. Poverty does not bless God. It does not bless you. It does not bless the world. Your poverty cannot bless the poor or the homeless. God despises poverty. Why would He want His children to have less than the best?

But thou shalt remember the Lord thy God: for it is he that giveth thee power to get wealth, that he may establish his covenant which he sware unto thy fathers, as it is this day.

Deuteronomy 8:18

You will be a leader in all things. Your wisdom will be sought after. You will no longer be the brunt of anyone's jokes. You will possess the wisdom of God, and you will have a ready answer for those seeking direction.

God will set you above all men. You will never again be beneath another man. God will establish your position. His Word will empower you. You will be established by God because you are grounded and founded in His Word.

I Want It All!

I don't want to miss even one of God's blessings. He has prepared them for those who love Him and who walk according to His Word.

There are even more blessings in the eleventh chapter of Deuteronomy and, as I said earlier, I want them as well. It reads:

> **Therefore shall ye keep all the commandments which I command you this day, that ye may be strong, and go in and possess the land, whither ye go to possess it;**
>
> **And that ye may prolong your days in the land, which the LORD sware unto your fathers to give unto them and to their seed....**
>
> **For the land, whither thou goest in to possess it, is not as the land of Egypt, from whence ye came out, where thou sowedst thy seed, and wateredst it with thy foot, as a garden of herbs:**
>
> **But the land, whither ye go to possess it, is a land of hills and valleys, and drinketh water of the rain of heaven:**
>
> **A land which the Lord thy God careth for: the eyes of the Lord thy God are always upon it, from the beginning of the year even unto the end of the year.**

And it shall come to pass, if ye shall hearken diligently unto my commandments which I command you this day, to love the Lord your God, and to serve him with all your heart and with all your soul,

That I will give you the rain of your land in his due season, the first rain and the latter rain, that thou mayest gather in thy corn, and thy wine, and thine oil.

And I will send grass in thy fields for thy cattle, that thou mayest eat and be full...Therefore shall ye lay up these my words in your heart and in your soul, and bind them for a sign upon your hand, that they may be as frontlets between your eyes.

And ye shall teach them your children, speaking of them when thou sittest in thine house, and when thou walkest by the way, when thou liest down, and when thou risest up.

And thou shalt write them upon the door posts of thine house, and upon thy gates:

That your days may be multiplied, and the days of your children, in the land which the Lord sware unto your fathers to give them, as the days of heaven upon the earth.

For if ye shall diligently keep all these commandments which I command you, to do them, to love the Lord your God, to walk in all his ways, and to cleave unto him;

Then will the Lord drive out all these nations from before you, and ye shall possess greater nations and mightier than yourselves.

Every place whereon the soles of your feet shall tread shall be yours....

There shall no man be able to stand before you: for the Lord your God shall lay the fear of you and the dread of you upon all the land that ye shall tread upon, as he hath said unto you.

Behold, I set before you this day a blessing and a curse;

A blessing, if ye obey the commandments of the Lord your God, which I command you this day.

Deuteronomy 11:8-27

When we get so full of God's Word that we speak it day and night, blessings will be ours. When there is nothing but the Word of God on our tongue, we will be abundantly blessed. When our mind becomes so filled with His Word, we will find the flow of God's blessings overtaking us.

If you feel like a spiritual weakling, just remember: power is a promise. You can be strong and possess the land. It is a promised blessing of God for walking in obedience.

You can march into the enemy's territory and possess what is rightfully yours. But you must know the power of God's Word living within you, and you must boldly walk in the strength of that Word.

You will live long to enjoy all the blessings of God if you have been abiding in His Word. You will possess strength and health as you have been directed by the commandments of God to care for your physical body. The Word of God is life.

You will possess a better land than you have known before. You will never again have to tolerate the conditions of the past. Once you move into, dwell in and abide in God's Word, you will find that even your surroundings have changed.

You will receive the Holy Ghost rain when you need it. It will be available to you at all times. The sweet moisture and covering of the anointing will come just when needed most. It is the commanded blessing of God.

When you receive the blessing of the anointing, your harvest will be abundant. You will bear much fruit as you are operating in God's Word. You can't predict it or order it — it comes in due season.

By living according to the Word, you will experience a little bit of heaven right here on earth. Your joy will be full, and you will have the peace that passes all understanding. (John 15:11; Phil. 4:7.) Now what could be more like heaven than that?

You will take dominion over your enemies, and not one will be able to defeat you. Your life in God will cause them to tremble with fear.

The blessing of God is everything we could ever hope for. Everyone wants joy, peace, prosperity and victory in their lives. The Church has gone to great lengths to get what it wants from God. We have expected Him to honor His promises to us, yet we have been unwilling to honor His Word with our obedience.

Instead of allowing God to command His blessing upon us, we have been commanding Him. To satisfy our fleshly desires, we have thrown His Word back in His face. Just as the devil tried to manipulate God with the Word, we have been playing the same game.

This is control. It is called manipulation, and manipulation is nothing but witchcraft. When you attempt to control another's thoughts or actions — no matter what device you are using — it is witchcraft.

Samuel spoke strongly to Saul when he reminded the king that **to obey is better than sacrifice....For rebellion is as the sin of witchcraft, and stubbornness is as iniquity and idolatry. Because thou hast rejected the word of the Lord, he hath also rejected thee from being king** (1 Sam. 15:22,23).

Saul's big mistake was failing to obey the commands God gave him when he was anointed king. At one point he was so desperate for direction that he even sought the counsel of a witch.

Saul already had God's Word on the matter; he didn't need a second opinion. God's directive was more than just an option; it was the law. Just like the Church today, Saul was looking for a more pleasing opinion — a better idea.

Paul warned Timothy and the New Testament Church about running to hear different teachers because of the problem of itching ears. (2 Tim. 4:3,4.) Some in the Church today have that same hearing problem. Suffering from selective hearing loss, they want a word that will be more to their liking and lifestyle. They seek teachers who will tell them what they want to hear.

We may be tossed by every wind of doctrine that blows through the Body of Christ, but God is not moved. He is still God and does not change. He is the same yesterday, today and forever. (Heb. 13:8.)

When we study the Word of God we are not reading a book filled with antiquated laws. We are reading a live, up-to-date message of love from our Creator.

God's written Word is clear. If you have a problem understanding it, there are hundreds of versions that make it plain. There are books and tape series that help to explain it.

Week after week, pastors enter their pulpits, rightly dividing the Word of Truth. There is no reason to misunderstand it, no excuse for disobeying it. It is God's Word.

Because I believe His Word, I live it. Because I love the Lord with all my heart, I live in His Word. As I learn His nature, I take it on.

Covet the Anointing

By studying the Word, you will better understand your place in the Body of Christ. You will recognize the importance of dwelling in that Word. The more you get, the more you will want.

Your hunger and appetite will increase as you grow. You will thirst for more and more of God. You will covet the power available to you through His Word. By the washing of the water of the Word over your soul, you will see yourself cleansed.

Ho, every one that thirsteth, come ye to the waters....

Incline your ear, and come unto me: hear, and your soul shall live; and I will make an everlasting covenant with you....

Seek ye the Lord while he may be found, call ye upon him while he is near:

Let the wicked forsake his way, and the unrighteous man his thoughts: and let him return unto the Lord, and he will have mercy upon him; and to our God, for he will abundantly pardon.

For my thoughts are not your thoughts, neither are your ways my ways, saith the Lord....

So shall my word be that goeth forth out of my mouth: it shall not return unto me void, but it shall accomplish that which I please, and it shall prosper in the thing whereto I sent it.

For ye shall go out with joy, and be led forth with peace....

Isaiah 55:1-12

As you seek Him, the Word becomes light and the darkened corners of your life are revealed. Your longing to be like Christ will send you scurrying to sweep out everything that is not like Him.

You will find out why you have been so slow to change. You will come to know why your stubborn will has hung on so long. You will begin to hate anything in you that is not like Jesus. As you struggle to overcome your flesh, you will find the power that is available through the Holy Ghost.

Once you discover the difference the Holy Spirit can make in your life, you will covet the anointing more than gold or silver. It will become rare and precious to you. The price is costly, but it is worth paying whatever it takes to have that covering on your life and ministry.

You will begin to see yourself as part of the Body of Christ. The Holy Spirit will reveal to you the importance of your part. Recognizing your worth, you will fulfill your responsibilities as directed by God's Word.

Once you have recognized that His Word was given just for you, the impact of such love will overwhelm you. You will realize the blood of His Son was shed just for you. Then it won't matter if you are a hand or a foot. You will forget *what* you are, because you will be caught up in *Whose* you are. Living in His love makes it easy to obey His every Word.

In the book of Acts when the Church was filled with the Holy Ghost, the people became of one heart and one soul. (Acts 4:32.) The power of the Spirit of God living within them gave them a corporate perspective. They no longer saw the things they possessed as their own, but they considered all things common.

The blessings that came on the heels of that experience were great power and grace, and great fear. This fear was not fright but an awesome sense of the power that was in God and available to them.

With their newly infused faith they saw great miracles and great wonders take place. Most importantly their unity gave them a powerful strength to face the persecutions that lay ahead.

As they listened to the Word of God that came through Philip, they were in one accord. They paid attention to that Word and saw miracles. Great joy overcame them as they watched God's power operate in accordance with His Word.

Do you want to be part of the Church that is about to receive the commanded blessing of God? True born-again, Spirit-filled, Word-dwelling, Bible-obeying saints are a minority. The day is coming when you will have to know what you believe and why you believe it. You will have to take a stand.

If you could not stand and obey the Word of God when it was popular to be a Christian, how will you stand when persecution comes? If you can't come into unity now with your brothers and sisters in Christ, how will you do it when the pressure is applied?

The Word is not frightening when you recognize it was given for protection, provision and peace. It was sent from a perfect God to the Body He loved. How then could His Word ever be grievous? He stands ready to perform His Word for those He loves. (Luke 1:45.)

You will only grieve over the Word when it is in conflict with your flesh. When you want your own way more than you want God's way, the way will be hard. It would be better never to have known the truth of the Word than to transgress the Word.

Now that you know the truth, what will you do? You want all God has for you, but you thought it would be easier to attain. You didn't know it would cost you so much. You didn't count on having to die to self.

You probably didn't consider that you were hindering the will of God for the Body of Christ. Here it is now, in black and white, and you must face it. What are you going to do with what you now know? Jesus tells us:

> If ye abide in me, and my words abide in you, ye shall ask what ye will, and it shall be done unto you.
>
> Herein is my Father glorified, that ye bear much fruit; so shall ye be my disciples.

As the Father hath loved me, so have I loved you: continue ye in my love.

If ye keep my commandments, ye shall abide in my love; even as I have kept my Father's commandments, and abide in his love.

These things have I spoken unto you, that my joy might remain in you, and that your joy might be full.

This is my commandment, That ye love one another, as I have loved you.

Greater love hath no man than this, that a man lay down his life for his friends.

Ye are my friends, if ye do whatsoever I command you.

Henceforth I call you not servants; for the servant knoweth not what his lord doeth: but I have called you friends; for all things that I have heard of my Father I have made known unto you.

Ye have not chosen me, but I have chosen you, and ordained you, that ye should go and bring forth fruit, and that your fruit should remain: that whatsoever ye shall ask of the Father in my name, he may give it to you.

These things I command you, that ye love one another.

John 15:7-17

If you love God, you will keep His commandments.

If you love your brothers and sisters, you will not sow discord.

Love will cause you to come into the unity that is demanded, then you will receive the blessing that is commanded.

It is God's Word. Believe it...obey it...receive from it!

About the Author

Rod Parsley began his ministry as an energetic 19 year old, in the backyard of his parent's Ohio home. The fresh, "old-time Gospel" approach of Parsley's delivery immediately attracted a hungry, God-seeking audience. From the 17 people who attended that first backyard meeting, the crowds grew rapidly.

Today, as the pastor of Columbus, Ohio's, 5200-seat World Harvest Church, Parsley oversees World Harvest's preschool-12 Christian Academy; World Harvest Bible College; and numerous church-sponsored outreaches and Breakthrough, World Harvest Church's daily and weekly television broadcast, currently heard by a potential audience of over 100 million people.

Rod Parsley also serves as Dr. Lester Sumrall's personal assistant in directing the End-Time Joseph "Feed the Hungry" program.

To contact the author
write:
Rod Parsley
World Harvest Church
P. O. Box 32932
Columbus, OH 43232

*Please include your prayer requests
and comments when you write.*

Books by Rod Parsley

Repairers of the Breach

My Promise is the Palace,
So What am I Doing in the Pit?

The Backside of Calvary

God's Answer to Insufficient Funds

Tribulation to Triumph

Holiness: Living Leaven Free

Praise and Worship

Serious Survival Strategies for Victory

Financial Abundance

If God Hadn't Wanted to Heal You, He Shouldn't Have

New Direction

Available from:

World Harvest Church
P. O. Box 32932
Columbus, OH 43232 U.S.A.